RETHINKING RETIREMENT

How to Create the Life You Want Without Waiting to Retire

by

Keith J. Weber, CFP®

Cover Art
by Capri Brock

A Books To Believe In Publication

Proudly Published in the USA by
Thornton Publishing, Inc
17011 Lincoln Ave. #408
Parker, CO 80134

Phone: 303.794.8888
Fax: 720.863.2013

EarlyRetirementHelp.com
Retirement2020.com
Rethinking-Retirement.com

ISBN: 0-9845417-2-1

Contents

Many people die with their music still in them. Why is this so? Too often it is because they are always getting ready to live. Before they know it, time runs out.

- Oliver Wendell Holmes

Chapter 1

Why Wait?

Several years ago I sat down with a couple to help them plan their retirement. Jeff[1] was a schoolteacher and Linda worked in retail sales. As we talked, I learned that Jeff was covered by a state pension program that used the "Magic 75" formula where he would qualify for full retirement benefits when his age and years of service combine to equal 75. At age 52 with 17 years of service, he was just a few years away. You can imagine my surprise then, when he responded to my question, "When would you like to retire?" by saying, "I want to leave at the end of this year."

"But why?" I asked. "You're so close to being able to retire with full benefits."

Without missing a beat he said, "Keith, I just don't love the little bastards anymore."

The unfortunate reality is that today, millions of people are miserable in their jobs. Some are merely restless and dissatisfied while others, well, the phrase "going postal" comes to mind. According to Marcia Bench, founder of the Career Coach institute, over 60% of workers today are dissatisfied with their current employment. While in a down economy many of us feel lucky even to have jobs, if given a choice, many of us would leave those jobs to do something we truly enjoy. Unfortunately, we often feel we have no other choice. Financially we are so immediately dependent on our current paycheck that the prospect of being without a paycheck or potentially earning less somewhere else is simply too big a risk to take.

But for millions of others, we stay in these jobs because we assume that doing so is the fastest path to creating the life we

[1] All client names and personal details have been changed.

really want to live. We've come to believe that we have to retire before we can finally do what we've always wanted. Over the years countless clients have told me they don't want to retire so they can sit around and do nothing. They want to retire so they can finally do what they've always wanted to do! Even those of us who enjoy our jobs often look forward to one day being able to retire - but not to the retirement of our grandfathers.

Over the years the concept of retirement has evolved. The dictionary's definition of retirement as a time "to withdraw" clearly no longer fits. Today we view retirement as a rebirth and a second chance, a time to re-engage in life and a time when anything is possible. We view retirement as a chance to recreate our lives exactly as we want them to be. That's the retirement we all look forward to. That's the dream that motivates so many of us to stay in the race.

Unfortunately, that dream is becoming harder and harder to achieve. With IRA and 401(k) account values down, home equity melting away, and, for private industry workers at least, pensions that have all but disappeared, achieving the retirement dream is becoming more and more elusive.

But it's not impossible.

In fact, the life you dream of at retirement may be achievable much sooner than you think. Creating that life means re-examining how we view our careers, work and even our perceptions of what retirement is. Specifically, creating the life you dream of at retirement can be yours today if you take these four steps.

First, we need to challenge some of our most basic assumptions - what I call myth-assumptions - that commonly pervade our thoughts about money, retirement and how our lives are "supposed" to go. Many of us hold certain beliefs that we've come to accept without ever really thinking about them. We grow up learning certain lessons, by watching what our parents, friends and co-workers do and hearing the constant drumming of various financial marketing messages on TV, radio and the internet. Eventually we come to believe that things are supposed to be done a certain way. The reality is that many of these assumptions no longer work in today's world. We need to look at these assumptions with a critical eye and determine for ourselves if the assumptions we hold will really lead us to a better life, or if those assumptions may in fact be holding us back from achieving the life we want.

Second, we need to start looking at our lives in a more holistic sense. One of the great ironies in life is that true happiness seldom comes from a single source, but it can be blocked by a single source. Having a great job, a large bank account or a passionately engaging interest will not create happiness if your health is poor or your family life is in shambles. We need to achieve balance and fulfillment in all areas of our lives. Traditional retirement planning continues to focus solely on the financial aspects, as if having enough money to lead the lifestyle of the rich and famous is enough to create a satisfying life. I can tell you from years of witnessing thousands of people firsthand, the threats to our happiness can come from any aspect of our lives and money does not solve all of these problems. We need to begin consciously looking at those other areas to identify and mitigate those threats before they become real.

Third, we need to clearly identify what we would like our lives to be. What are our true values and priorities? What is it we really want out of life? Only when we discover our deepest and truest answer to that question will we find lasting satisfaction.

Finally, we need to learn to manage our financial resources for maximum benefit in meeting our true values and priorities. Too many of us believe that if we just had little bit more money all of our problems would be solved. After 20 years in the financial services industry I can tell you that no matter how much you have, "enough" is never enough. Not until we learn to make financial decisions based on supporting our true values and priorities will we ever feel confident in our financial security.

If all this sounds a little surprising or a little too soft to be coming from a serious retirement book, it might be helpful to know the results of a recent retirement survey. In January 2010, Merrill Lynch surveyed a group of retirees and found that 51% wished they would have spent more time focusing on their life goals, and not just on achieving their retirement "number" when preparing for retirement. As such, this book is arranged in two sections. The first part, Chapters 2 through 7, will deal with the softer side of defining your life goals, challenging various myth-assumptions and creating a vision of your ideal life. The second part, Chapters 8-12, will examine some of the hard skills needed to manage your money in a way that allows you to make that life real.

If that still doesn't answer the question as to why a guy who spent 20 years as a financial advisor crunching the numbers and doing analysis is writing a book about the softer side of retirement, perhaps hearing my own story will help.

A Wake-Up Call

I began my financial services career in 1988, just a year after the now-infamous Black Monday stock market crash of 1987. Like millions of others just a year out of college, I was trying to find my place in the world and struggling to make ends meet. When a friend suggested I interview with a stock brokerage firm that was hiring, I decided to give it a shot.

In the early years things were pretty lean. At the time there were few formal, comprehensive training programs for financial advisors, so most of the training came on the job. This being the late 1980s however, it wasn't necessarily financial advisor training, but rather sales training that a new advisor received. In fact, I learned more about being a financial advisor by observing what *not* to do from other advisors than I ever did from any of the so-called training I received.

Recognizing I needed a more comprehensive education, I enrolled in the College for Financial Planning and by the mid-1990s obtained the Certified Financial Planner™ designation. With that came greater confidence, credibility, and a better ability to truly serve my clients. With all of that in place, my practice began to grow nicely. In fact, as my client list, revenues and overall practice continued to flourish, I began to receive national recognition. Even though the segment of the industry I worked in, banks and credit unions, was a small niche within the overall industry, I had become a pretty big fish within that small pond.

As the years progressed, however, the doubts began to creep in. For all the people I was helping and all the success I was having, it just didn't feel like enough. As happens with every job, I had days where I felt good about the job I was doing, and days where I felt I was banging my head against a wall. Unfortunately those "head-banging" days seemed to be outnumbering the good ones by a fairly wide margin. The job that at one time had been so engaging and fun was now stressful and frustrating. I began to feel hollow inside and to ask myself, "Is this it? Is this what all the hard work is for?"

I began to realize that I, like so many of my clients, had become one of the "walking wounded," sleepwalking through my days at a job that was at best merely tolerable. But like so many others, I had bought into and even perpetuated the belief that the only reason we work today is so that someday when we retire, we won't have to work anymore. Financial independence and the ability to retire were the ultimate goals not only for me, but for my clients and millions of others caught up in the race. Now only in my late 30s however, retirement seemed a long way off.

Unfortunately I also had another problem. I was afflicted with a condition that millions of others also suffer with that I call the accumulation addiction - the feeling that no matter how much you have, it's never enough. Accumulation addiction is the belief that if I can just accumulate a little more, *then* I'll be OK. So even though I was growing restless and dissatisfied with my career, the idea of changing careers seemed too much of a risk. I assumed I would never make the kind of money I was making now, and even if I could it would take years to make up the lost earnings. "No," I thought, "it's better to keep my head down and keep striving for that financial independence. When I retire," I thought (just like my clients), "then I'll finally be able to do what I've always wanted." So I did what millions of others both before and after me have done – I started working even harder. I took on even more responsibilities, worked still longer hours, made even more money and became even less satisfied.

It all came to a head (literally) one day when I was rushing to the airport to catch a flight home after a week's worth of meetings and travel. For several weeks I had been dealing with a persistent headache that I thought was the result of a simple cold. As I descended the hillside on Highway 380 leading to San Francisco International Airport, the slight change in air pressure caused my ears to pop, and I felt the strangest sensation emerge from the top of my head. It was as if someone had just poured electrically charged molasses over me. Slowly a tingling sensation eased down from the top of my head, across my face, down my neck and eventually down my arms, torso and legs until my entire body tingled. My arms felt frozen in place until I was afraid I wouldn't be able to control the car. Slowly the tingling faded and I pulled over to the side of the freeway until I was able to pull myself together.

The next week I went to see my doctor and told him of this experience, which puzzled him as much as it had me. The rest of my symptoms seemed consistent with a cold that had been going around, so he gave me a prescription and told me to come back if things hadn't cleared up in a couple of weeks. Two weeks later, the cold was gone, but the headache persisted, so we tried another prescription. A month after that, the headache was still there, so he suggested a CAT scan. By now, the holidays were upon us so I took some time between Christmas and New Year's to have the scan.

Shortly after the New Year, I received a call from my doctor's office asking me to come in and discuss the results of my scan. "That's odd," I thought. "Normally they just tell you everything is negative and you go about your business." When I went to see my doctor after work that evening, he told me in a matter-of-fact kind of voice, "Keith, you have a brain tumor."

I don't remember much of the conversation beyond that point. I recall him saying something about this type of tumor almost always being benign, but that I should have an MRI and have a specialist take a look at it just in case. There was something about based on my age, the location and size of the tumor, he thought it likely a specialist would recommend having it removed, but I wasn't really listening. Instead, my thoughts immediately turned to the wife of a good friend of mine, Cathy, who had just six months earlier also discovered she had a brain tumor. Everything for her had turned out fine. She had surgery to remove the tumor and was back to her old self within just a few months. With my doctor's matter-of-fact attitude and having just witnessed Cathy's successful outcome, I wasn't initially overly concerned.

In fact, as sick as this sounds, I actually felt *relief*. I finally had an excuse to take some time off and step away from the rat race. I had become so stressed and had been putting in such long hours that initially I actually looked forward to the surgery. I had plenty of sick leave built up and now had the perfect excuse to use a good chunk of it. According to my doctor there was nothing to worry about. They would just cut a hole, reach in and lift it out. It's simple, nothing to worry about, right? That is, until I started doing some research.

As I began to read more and more about the type of tumor I had, a meningioma, I realized it was actually a very common tumor. As a doctor friend of mine told me, "If you're going to have a brain tumor, that's the kind to have." Frighteningly however, I discovered they don't always come one at a time; they like to show up in groups of two or three. As I sought out various opinions and support groups, I found several others in my community who had also been diagnosed with this type of tumor. For some, their experiences were very casual, a bump in the road from which they soon recovered. For others, it had lasting implications that impacted their lives on a daily basis. The more I learned, the more apprehensive I became. Chances were very good my outcome would be positive, but by now I had learned enough to know that wasn't always the case.

As I gathered various medical opinions, the overall consensus was that while everyone agreed the tumor should be removed, the timing was not urgent. This was a slow-growing, almost always benign tumor. As long as I had it removed within the next few months everything should be fine. So before going in, my wife and I decided to take a trip to Hawaii with Cathy and her husband. While we visited the island of Kauai, the four of us decided to go zip-lining – live for today, right? We each strapped into a harness and attached ourselves to long cables stretched between the valley walls. As we stepped from the platform, gravity and our momentum sent us flying above the canopy of a tropical jungle. Time after time we flew through the trees high above the valley floor. Midway through the day, we stopped for lunch at a perfect little tropical waterfall that plunged 20 feet into a pool of crystal clear water. As our guides prepared lunch, we climbed to the top of the waterfall and dove repeatedly into the pool. As I watched Cathy dive into the pool a moment of peace came over me. Here she was, just months after having brain surgery and now living life to the fullest. In that moment, I knew everything was going to be all right. I *knew* the surgery was going to go well. I knew I would be fine. It wasn't a feeling of confidence, faith or hope, it was a conviction I felt deep within my being. At that moment I *knew* this tumor would not get the best of me.

As I recovered at home after the surgery I had a lot of time to think about my life. The little voice that had asked "Is this it?" seemed a little less persistent, as if its message was finally sinking in. Here I was with a very successful career, but virtually no outside interests. I spent what little free time I had with my family - which was great - but between that and work I had very little social life or other hobbies. I needed to create some balance in my life but knew that would be difficult with the demands of my current job. For several years I had considered striking out on my own and if I ever expected there to be a sign from the universe telling me when to make the move, this seemed to be it. A few weeks before I was scheduled to return to work, I called my boss and resigned.

You would think this would be the turning point of the story, right? Unfortunately it is not. The accumulation addiction still held a strong grip on me. A few months after I resigned, my old boss called me up with a proposal. He had accepted a job as CEO with a new company and wanted me to join him on his executive management team at the new firm. Although the salary was actually less than I had been making before, he offered an equity stake in the new privately-held firm that had the potential to be quite lucrative. With the accumulation addiction as strong as ever, the opportunity seemed too good to pass up, so I dove back in.

But like many things that start out so promising, this new job quickly descended into something far worse than I had ever experienced. I was soon traveling 3-4 weeks every month, actually spending more nights in hotels that first year than I did at home. The rat race seemed to find a new gear and in my heart I knew I had sold out. Life had given me a wake-up call and I hit the snooze button. Instead of taking the opportunity to get my priorities in order and make lasting changes, I had fallen back into the same old routine. Instead of following my heart to create the life I wanted, I had succumbed to the accumulation addiction and jumped back in. The universe it seemed, had actually spoken to me, but I failed to listen, and now I was paying for it.

Fortunately, a second, less severe wake-up call came one day when I had the rare opportunity to be at home for a full week. Toward the end of the week I asked my wife if I could pick up our two boys from school or how else I could help. She looked at me with eyes full of love and understanding but just a hint of frustration in her voice and said, "We love that you're home, but you're disrupting our routine. We've done it long enough without you that it's actually easier when you're gone."

Ouch.

At that moment I knew I had my priorities backwards. Not only was I sacrificing my relationships with the people who were most important to me, but also with all those who had supported me during my earlier crisis. Rather than spending my time nurturing those relationships and pursuing work that was personally meaningful, I was spending it in airports, hotels, and in the pursuit of goals that weren't even mine.

Thankfully, it didn't take long after that to leave the corporate world for good.

Even though I'd been aware of the accumulation addiction in my clients, I had failed to see it in myself. The desire to accumulate more was not helping me to achieve the life I wanted; it was actually moving me further away. I was so focused on becoming financially independent in hopes of retiring at some point in the future that I failed to create a life in the present, and as a result I neglected those things that were truly most important to me. As I speak to various groups across the country, I realize I'm not alone.

Chapter 2

Do We Really Want to "Retire?"

Why is it that we are asked to make one of the most important decisions of our lives at a time when we are least prepared to do so? That decision of course, is what kind of career we want to go into. Very few 18-22 year olds have either the breadth of world experience or personal self-awareness to know what they want to do for the rest of their lives. And yet, as a 42 year-old dentist friend of mine once lamented, "Here I am stuck with my hands in people's mouths all day just because some 18 year-old idiot decided he wanted to be a dentist!"

It's one thing to simply be bored with your job, your boss or any other element of your current employment. It's quite another to feel, as Stephen Covey, author of *The 7 Habits of Highly Effective People,* so eloquently expressed, that your career ladder is against the wrong wall. A study by AARP found that while over 80% of Baby Boomers plan on continuing to work in some capacity during retirement, over 55% plan to be in an entirely different field, career or industry. Today we don't view retirement as the end of our productive lives, we view it as an opportunity to put our ladders against the right wall and finally do what we've always wanted to do.

Why So Many Ladders are Against the Wrong Walls

How is it that so many of us end up in jobs we can't wait to retire away from? Certainly no one ever chooses to go into a job they think they'll be miserable at, but millions of us end up that way. For most of my clients, there were four reasons.

1. ***Economic necessity followed by career complacency.*** Let's face it, many of us, at various points throughout our working lives, have been forced to take jobs that we knew from the beginning weren't an ideal fit for us. It might have been due to layoffs within a tight job market, financial obligations or any number of other personal circumstances, but many of us have taken jobs we viewed as temporary until "something better comes along." Over time we become comfortable with the job, we settle in and perhaps even begin to moderately enjoy what we're doing. After a raise or two the money begins to look a little better than what we might find elsewhere, so we stick it out. If we had dreams about what our ideal job would be, we often tend to forget them as our attention and focus is drawn to other areas of our lives. Especially for those of us who were not able to land a job within our ideal career path when we initially entered the workforce, getting back on the right track becomes increasingly difficult. We get married, have children and take on a mortgage. Slowly but steadily we begin to rely more and more on that steady paycheck to support the life we've built, while our dreams slowly fade away. Before we know it a decade or two has gone by and the dreams of our youth have become nothing but distant memories.

2. ***Taking a wrong turn.*** Many of us start off on the right path, but in our effort to climb the corporate ladder we grab the wrong rung. Not only was I a great example of that when I followed my ex-boss to his new company, but I saw countless other examples among my clients. One client named Ed was a particularly good example. A successful engineer by training, Ed had aggressively pursued several promotions and over time had come to manage a division of well over 500 people. Only after taking several steps up the corporate ladder did Ed unfortunately discover that managing others was not his forte. Not that he wasn't good at it, he just

didn't enjoy the endless meetings, the tiresome personnel issues and never-ending office politics. He missed the hands-on work of designing and the feeling of accomplishment that came with it. Like so many of us, Ed started off on the right path, but made a wrong turn along the way.

3. ***The job itself changes.*** In this era of mergers and acquisitions, reorganizations and restructurings, even if you've been fortunate enough to find the perfect job, things often change. A good friend of mine in the financial services industry thought he had the perfect job, until his firm merged with another. The resulting changes in operating systems, paperwork requirements and what he considered nonsensical internal bureaucratic requirements turned what was a great job that he enjoyed tremendously into one that he couldn't wait to get away from. When the changes are large and sudden, it's easy to see what's happening. But when the changes are small, as most of them are, the cumulative effect is a slow transformation from a job or career that was at one time satisfying and fulfilling to one that's become dull and tedious. We become like the proverbial frog in the pan of boiling water. If dumped into the boiling water immediately, we'll sense the change and jump right back out. But put us into cool water and allow the heat to gradually rise, we'll stay put until we boil to death. Depending on what stage in their career people find themselves when this happens, many will choose to wait it out until retirement instead of leaving to find a better situation.

4. ***We change.*** Probably the biggest reason many of us are less satisfied with our jobs than we used to be is that what motivates us may have changed. Early in our careers we are often driven by the desire to succeed, to earn more money or to achieve a position of responsibility and influence. As we mature, our

personal priorities change. Now we may begin to feel the need to create balance in our lives, to contribute in a socially meaningful way, or to accomplish something more. Suddenly the idea of making more money and having more responsibilities is overcome by the desire to simplify and make a difference.

Maslow 101

This fact - that the drivers that motivate us to take certain actions change within us over time - lies at the heart of the conflict so many of us feel as we hold out for retirement. As such, we need to look a little closer at what's really going on.

In the mid-1900s, American psychologist Abraham Maslow introduced his hierarchy of human development, in which he saw human beings' needs arranged as a pyramid. Maslow suggested that the fulfillment of these needs is the driving, motivating force behind all human activities. Everything we do is driven by our desire to fulfill these needs.

As you can see in figure 2.1, Maslow placed our most basic survival needs for air, food, water and shelter, at the bottom of the pyramid. As our most fundamental needs, these must be met first before we concern ourselves with anything else. As children, our parents typically satisfy these needs for us. When we strike out into the world on our own as young adults, finding a place to live and a means to put groceries on the table are our most pressing concerns. As we meet these needs and establish our economic foothold, we then move on.

On the second level, Maslow placed the need for safety, security and stability, followed on the third tier by the psychological or social needs for love, belonging and acceptance. Again, as young adults we seek to find jobs that are not only engaging, but also provide a steady income. We fall in love, get married, start a family and establish a place within our communities, thereby satisfying our second and third level needs.

The fourth level of the pyramid includes the need to fulfill our self-esteem through achievement, accomplishment and by garnering the respect of others. As our careers progress throughout our late 20s and on into our early 40s, these needs for status and esteem are often filled by our career accomplishments.

Figure 2.1 -
Maslow's Hierarchy of Human Development

Finally at the top, Maslow placed what he termed the self-actualizing needs. Maslow described self-actualization as the achievement of our fullest potential in the service of something greater than ourselves. To be truly happy and fulfilled, he suggested, we must be engaged in those activities that we are deeply called to do, and sense that those activities have meaning and impact beyond just ourselves. Typically occurring in our 40s or 50s, the evolution of these very natural and innate human needs causes our priorities and values to shift away from a career focus to more personally satisfying endeavors. Today, in our modern, three-life-stage culture, we view retirement as the time we can finally pursue those endeavors.

Evolution of the Retirement Concept

Prior to the creation of Social Security in 1935, the typical American's life was defined in two stages - education and work. Except for the railroads and a handful of other forward-thinking organizations, very few retirement pension programs existed. With the creation of Social Security as a formal public pension program, retirement became the accepted third "life stage" following a person's career. But for most Americans prior to 1935, retirement wasn't an option.

To understand further, it helps to remember what life was like for the average American 100 years ago. Up until 1920, more Americans lived on farms than in the cities. Multiple generations of families lived in the same household and took care of one another as they aged. There were no nursing homes or retirement communities; families cared for one another. But as the Industrial Revolution kicked into high gear, younger people began following the jobs from the farms into the cities, leaving elder generations to fend for themselves.

Work too, was much more physically demanding back in those days. There were no combines and tractors to help with the harvest. Fields were plowed with the horse and the hoe. In the factories, there were no robotic arms or computerized assembly. It took brute physical labor to manufacture the products of the day. Workers, just like the machines they worked with, were considered just another part of the assembly line that produced the products. Eventually those parts wore out and had to be replaced.

In fact, the Social Security system was not created for the primary purpose of caring for or providing a benefit to older workers. Although certainly marketed that way, its real purpose was to provide a means to remove older workers from the workforce. Like cogs in a machine, people wore out. Younger workers were typically more capable of handling the physical demands of the job better than their older counterparts. With unemployment among young men soaring during the Great Depression of the 1930s, providing a system to remove older individuals from the workforce freed up jobs for younger, more productive workers. Social Security was a way to remove those older workers.

As a result, retirement in the 1930s, 1940s and even into the 1950s wasn't viewed as something to look forward to, but rather it was the very public recognition that one's productivity and ability to contribute was all used up. It was like publicly admitting you had nothing left to give to the world. Retirement wasn't something to be celebrated, but rather marked the end of one's productive life. It was perceived as having one foot already in the grave.

But slowly over time, as advances in technology made the work less physically demanding, our overall health at age 65 - the long-held "normal" retirement age established by the Social Security Act in 1935 - improved. For those who retired in the 1960s and 70s, this was a time of great confusion and frustration. These folks had more to contribute, their usefulness far from used up. But socially, the stigma stuck. Once you reached age 65, you were expected to retire, to make way for the next generation. Many of my clients related stories of their grandfathers, whittling away the time in their rocking chairs on the front porch, essentially waiting to die. This was the generation that spawned so many anecdotal stories of someone retiring from a long career, and dying shortly thereafter. As became apparent to many of these grandchildren in the years that followed, their grandparents did not necessarily die from ill health (well OK- that was obviously a big part of it) but rather from a loss of the will to live.

It wasn't until the 1980s that the "golden years" of retirement began to be viewed as a vibrant and active time in a person's life. (Remember the *Golden Girls*?) Now, retirement began to be viewed as a 20-30 year vacation. Not only was it a reward for a lifetime of hard work, but it also came to be viewed as a basic right, an entitlement, something that we had earned and was owed to us. This was the first generation that had spent their entire working life contributing through Social Security taxes to other people's retirement. Now it was their turn, and they were going to make the most of it.

Making the most of it in the 1980s and early 90s however, meant that retirement was viewed as a time of no work and all play. Retirement represented the good life and became the life goal for millions of workers. Whereas in the 1980s the social mantra had been "He who dies with the most wins," by the 1990s that mantra had become "He who retires first, wins!" Early retirement was seen as a sign of career and personal success. Companies like IBM, Eastman Kodak, Hewlett Packard, General Motors and more began offering extremely lucrative early retirement packages. And not just to the executives, but to many of the rank-and-file employees. Early retirement became a reality for many people who were only in their early to mid-50s.

But an interesting thing then happened. A series of studies were conducted in the early 2000s that began to look into just how happy these early retirees were. One study led by the University of Michigan, looked at people who had retired early, defined as before age 59 ½, and had been retired for at least five years. They asked these early retirees if they were happier now that they had been retired for five years, or if they were happier before they retired. Over 60% indicated they were actually happier before they retired!

As they dug a little deeper, they found that of the 40% who said they were happier after retiring, the majority of them had gone on to engage in some kind of meaningful activity. Some went back to work, others volunteered, and others became caregivers for members of their family. Almost universally, those who were happier after retiring had found a meaningful purpose in their lives.

On the other hand, of the 60% who indicated they had been happier before they retired, the majority of them had taken the idea that retirement is a time of leisure and ease to heart. They had not become engaged in any meaningful activities, they had lost touch with friends and saw a diminishing social circle, and reported frequent boredom and depression.

The study concluded what psychologists have been telling us for years - and something that most of us instinctively know - people need a purpose. We need to feel productive and needed. We need to feel as if our lives matter and that we are capable of contributing to those around us. As a result, our ideas of what we perceive the ideal retirement to be has evolved yet again.

Long gone are the days of retirement being associated with rocking chairs, but so too is the idea of retirement being a time of complete ease and leisure - the so-called "30-year vacation." Today we view retirement as a time in our lives when anything is possible, when we can shake off the shackles of financial worry and personal responsibility and follow our hearts to live lives that are meaningful and fulfilling. Exactly what we'll do to create that meaning and fulfillment is often unclear, but we associate the term retirement and that stage of our lives as a time of rebirth to discover exactly what that may be. As a result of this almost mythical image we've created around it, retirement has become *the* life goal and *the* destination for millions of workers.

FDR Meets Maslow

It's taken us a half century to get here, but today we view retirement as a time of self-actualization. Although few of us will actually use that term, we now view retirement as the time to finally do those things we've been deeply called to do. Recognizing that fact helps us to better understand the struggle that so many of us face in striving toward retirement and the solution to the work/retirement dilemma.

One of the stipulations to progressing to the higher levels on Maslow's hierarchy is that all the previous needs lower on the pyramid must be met and maintained first. Maslow felt that lower-level unfulfilled needs would inhibit the person from climbing to the next step. If someone has met a need and moved upward, only to have that lower-level need suddenly reappear, then according to Maslow, the person's attention and energy would be redirected back down toward that no longer satisfied lower-level need until it was once again met. Only when those needs were once again satisfied could they then resume their previous higher level. As he succinctly pointed out, someone dying of thirst quickly forgets their thirst when they have no oxygen.

Interestingly though, Maslow also suggested that once glimpsed, the higher-level needs never truly go away - they are simply suspended for the time being until the lower-level need is once again satisfied. It's like tasting your favorite dessert. If you've never had it, you don't know what you're missing. But once you've tasted it, you'll always want to come back for more.

This caveat - that needs lower on the pyramid must be met and maintained prior to moving on to higher levels and that higher-level needs, once realized, never go away - is important for understanding how the concept of retirement has evolved over the years. As our society has advanced, it has become easier to meet our lower-level needs. As discussed, not only has the work become less physically demanding, but improved distribution networks and increased disposable income (as compared to 50 years ago) have made most basic, survival goods easily accessible. Whereas 100 years ago the majority of Americans still lived on farms and had to work the fields to grow their own food simply to survive, today we easily go down to the corner market to purchase dinner. We don't haul water from the stream, we turn on a tap. The amount of energy we have to expend today to meet our physiological and safety needs is miniscule compared to 100 years ago.

The result is that today we move much more quickly up Maslow's pyramid than we ever did in the past. While our desire to find love and belonging still remains in our 20s, today we find esteem and status through career success in our 30s and sooner. By the time we reach our 40s and 50s, the drivers that motivated us early in our careers change. Instead of seeking wealth, power, status and achievement, we're now driven by a desire to simplify, to achieve balance in our lives and to make a difference in the world. We seek a strong sense of purpose and meaning, and we're ready to move on to the next stage of our personal development. According to Maslow, that next stage is self-actualization. According to FDR and our modern culture, the next stage is retirement.

Herein lies the source of this internal struggle. Emotionally, many of us are well ready to make changes in our lives long before we're financially able to retire. But with our need to continue to earn an income and the lure of this idealized retirement pulling us forward, we stay in those jobs hoping that one day we'll accumulate enough so that we can in fact retire, and only then finally create the life we want. This belief that we have to retire before we can finally create the life we want is the first of three myth-assumptions we'll address. My client Ed, whom I mentioned earlier, was a perfect example.

The Three Myth-Assumptions

Myth One:
I Have to Retire Before I Can Do What I've Always Wanted to Do

"I don't want to retire so that I can sit back and do nothing," Ed responded when I asked about his retirement plans. "I want to retire so I can finally do what I've always wanted to do." Over the 20 years that I have been helping people plan for retirement my clients have repeated that same refrain over and over again.

To put it bluntly, Ed couldn't wait to retire. Having taken a wrong turn on his climb up the corporate ladder, Ed now looked forward to retirement as his way out of a job that had become tedious drudgery. Retirement would finally allow him to spend all his time pursuing his true passion - photography. He loved nothing more than to spend hours watching and waiting for the perfect sunrise, sunset, or other wildlife photo opportunity. He'd converted a small room in his basement into a darkroom and then, with the evolution of digital photography, converted a second room to handle this new medium. In fact, by devoting only a few hours a week to his hobby, he'd actually begun to earn a nice little second income from selling his photos. Now, with a new goal in mind and the promise of retirement just a few years away (including a boatload of stock options soon to be vested), Ed set his sights firmly on retirement as his way out.

Unfortunately, the company had other plans. With business down during the aftermath of 9/11, Ed's company announced a series of "workforce management" events - layoffs - to occur as soon as possible. Ed came to see me when he learned he was about to be let go.

As we worked through his options, I was surprised to hear the direction Ed's job search was taking. Instead of looking at how he might ramp up his photography business, he was once again looking for an executive-level managerial job. When I asked him about this, his response seemed logical - he wanted to make the most money possible so he could still reach his goal of an early retirement. But the fact of the matter was, that with the severance, vacation pay, the immediate vesting of his stock options and other money he had saved, Ed had enough liquid cash on hand to support himself and his wife quite comfortably for the next two years without touching his retirement savings. Not only that, but the photo business was already bringing in about half of what he estimated he would need when he actually did retire. Starting a business is no small feat, but now seemed the perfect time to take that leap to see if he could build that hobby into a long-term, profitable, personally fulfilling venture.

"But what are you going to *do* when you retire?" I asked.

"That's when I'll ramp up the photography business." he responded.

"Why do you feel you need to wait?" I asked.

With that, Ed paused and sat back in his chair. "I guess," he said, "I've always thought that's what I was supposed to do. I mean, I'm 54 - too young to really retire. Shouldn't I be spending these next few years maxing my earnings so I can really retire when I'm 59?"

"That's certainly one option," I said. "But if you really enjoy your photography, what's to prevent you from continuing to earn an income doing that for the next 10 or 15 years? That will help you delay taking withdrawals from your retirement accounts, which will certainly help at least as much as continuing to contribute for the next five years."

Like so many of us, Ed had bought into the myth-assumption that we have to retire first, and only then can we do what we really want to do. He viewed retirement as a finish line, the end of the time in his life when he would spend his time doing what he felt he "had to" or "should" do, and the beginning of the time when he could finally do what he always wanted to do. Part of that belief was born out of Ed's strong work ethic instilled by his parents. "Get your work done first, then you can play," they told him. Never did it occur to them, to Ed, or to many of us, that work and play could be the same thing. With his background, photography gave him a way to use both his technical and artistic skills in a hands-on fashion. But to Ed, photography was a hobby. Even though he made several thousand dollars a year selling his photos part-time, he didn't see it as a legitimate career option.

Myth Two: Retirement Means Total Financial Freedom

The second myth-assumption about retirement is that financial freedom means being able to do whatever we want, whenever we want. Consider this: Most of us would agree that here in the United States we enjoy more freedom and more liberty than has been available in any other country at any other time in history. Yet we still have to follow certain rules. I can't yell "fire!" in a crowded theatre. I can't drive the wrong way down a one-way street (although admittedly, I have made that mistake once or twice...), and I can't take someone else's property. Even though we live in a free society, there are still rules and limitations on what we can and cannot do.

In the same way, financial freedom also comes with rules and limitations. One client I worked with many years ago interpreted his passage into retirement as carte blanche to spend whatever he wanted. The investment assets he had accumulated were more than sufficient to provide the monthly income he needed, but against my recommendation, every few months he kept making significant additional withdrawals from his principal. Over time his principal was drawn down to an amount that could no longer generate his required monthly income, and he was forced to go back to work.

Financial freedom, as we'll discuss in more detail in the coming chapters, does not mean being able to spend whatever we want, whenever we want. While most of us consciously "get it," subconsciously we associate retirement as a time of complete financial freedom and lack of limitations. As a result, we focus on accumulating as much as we can and sacrifice our current quality of life in hopes of one day being without those limitations.

Myth Three: This is How it's Supposed to Be

The third myth-assumption is the belief that this is just how our lives are supposed to go. When FDR signed the Social Security Act in 1935, he perhaps unknowingly charted the life path that millions of us would follow for decades to come. By formally creating a retirement program that would benefit everyone, he simultaneously created the three-life-stage roadmap of education, career and retirement that we've all come to accept. Over the years that roadmap has become so ingrained in our culture that we've come to believe that following those three stages is simply how our lives are "supposed" to go. We're supposed to get educated, have a long and hopefully rewarding career, then at age 65 or sooner settle in for a long and comfortable retirement.

While we may be very well justified in expecting a comfortable retirement, the reality is that it's getting more and more difficult to achieve.

Chapter 3

The Challenge to Baby Boomers and "Generation Jones"

For current and soon-to-be retirees, financial security in retirement has long been characterized as being supported by a three legged stool. The first leg represents Social Security, the second an employer's pension, and the third represents our own personal savings and investments. As we'll see, for all but the most leading-edge Baby Boomers, these traditional legs of the retirement stool have become so wobbly it simply isn't prudent to count solely on them to secure our long-term financial future.

Social Security

There's been a lot of talk regarding the future solvency of Social Security. The fact is that in 1950 the worker-to-beneficiary ratio was 16.5-to-1, meaning there were 16 and a half workers contributing through payroll taxes for each person receiving benefits. Today that ratio is 3.3-to-1, and within 40 years will fall to 2-to-1. According to Social Security's own web site, "at this ratio there will not be enough workers to pay scheduled benefits at current tax rates." In fact, even before the 2008-2009 downturn in the economy, the Trustees who oversee Social Security and Medicare had indicated that as early as 2017 the amount of money coming into Social Security through payroll taxes would no longer be enough to pay scheduled benefits. With higher unemployment due to the economic downturn and therefore fewer people paying in, the Congressional Budget Office has moved that date all the way up to this year and now forecasts that payouts will exceed collections by $29 billion here in 2010.

There are a number of people, however, who disregard the fact that Social Security will soon be paying out more than it takes in. These folks cite the fact that a Social Security Trust Fund exists that can pay benefits all the way until 2037. The problem is that these funds don't exist. Or to state it more accurately, these funds exist as IOUs. Over the years, as the U.S. Treasury has collected excess Social Security tax revenues, it has issued IOUs - essentially an accounting entry - to a ledger account referred to as the Social Security Trust Fund. Then, with Congressional approval, the Treasury has dumped these excess revenues into the Treasury's general fund and used them to fund other projects. The net result is that there is no real money in the Social Security Trust fund, just a bunch of accounting entries for IOUs. To collect on these IOUs, new revenues (taxes) need to be created not only to repay the loans, but to maintain the other programs that they initially funded as well.

To be realistic, I think it's prudent to emphasize that the likelihood of Social Security completely disappearing from our retirement landscape is remotely small. Changes are certain to be made, but the obligation we feel as a country to support our citizens as we age will ensure that a program of some kind will continue to be in place. To fix the current system however, there are really only two possible dials that can be adjusted: reduce benefits or increase income. Several options exist around each, but not surprisingly none of them are particularly popular. Benefits can be reduced to current recipients, or the age at which new recipients become eligible for benefits can be delayed. To increase income, payroll taxes can be raised, or the number of workers paying into the system can be increased. The most likely scenario is that modifications will be made to both sides of the equation, but even the slightest tinkering is likely to have serious consequences. For example:

- If benefits are reduced, each of us will be required to save more to support ourselves in retirement. Those in greatest need will have the least opportunity to do so, leading to an increase in the number of people living at or near poverty.

- If payroll taxes are increased, experts agree that the amount by which they would need to be raised would strain an already weakened economy and could likely send the US, and possibly the world, into an even deeper recession, if not a sustained depression. If that happens, we can reasonably assume the value of our personal investment accounts will also suffer, perhaps severely, further damaging our personal financial security.

- If the age of eligibility is increased, the date of economic emancipation is delayed. Each of us will need to work longer to support ourselves. This may be one of the most realistic options, but for those who are anxious to retire from a job they hate, this would be a major disappointment.

- Finally, increasing the number of workers who are paying in can be accomplished two ways. The most beneficial would be to decrease unemployment and put more people back to work. Obviously that's a challenge that the president and congress will continue to work on. Congress could also do away with separate government funded pensions and force those government workers who are not currently covered by Social Security to participate. Not surprisingly, that idea is not particularly popular among those who are covered by these separate pensions.

While these are the most likely alternatives that exist within the current system, they are not the only options. The other of course, is to abandon Social Security altogether and create a completely new system. The Economic Policy Institute and several others have suggested alternatives to end Social Security as we know it. In its place they propose the creation of everything from what are called Guaranteed Retirement Accounts - basically a government-run 401(k) with a pension-only distribution option - to a Private Security System with individual investment accounts. Regardless of which plan you might prefer, the divisive nature of these kinds of proposals ensures that they will be hotly debated before any corrective action is put in place.

Employer Pensions

The second leg of the traditional retirement income security stool is that of employer-sponsored pension plans. Since the enactment of ERISA (Employee Retirement Income Security Act) in 1974, the percentage of active workers covered by defined benefit (traditional pension) plans has declined substantially. Gone are the days of working 30 years for one company then retiring with a pension and a gold watch. The Department of Labor estimates that in 1980, about 40% of all private wage and salary workers in the U.S. were covered by some type of traditional pension plan. By 2004, the Bureau of Labor Statistics reports only 21% of current private industry workers were participating in such plans. Frighteningly, workers are not realizing this is happening. According to a 2007 study by the Employee Benefit Research Institute, 62% of workers still expect they will receive retirement income from a defined benefit pension plan, even though only 21% are actually covered.[2]

With the arrival of ERISA, the trend among employers has been unmistakably away from providing traditional defined benefit pension plans and toward defined contribution plans such as 401(k)s, 403(b)s, SEP-IRAs and the like. At first these defined contribution plans were hailed as giving the employees more control, allowing them the ability to save for themselves. Unfortunately, actual experience is proving that is not happening. Not only are participation rates low, but many employees lack the ability to effectively invest the money they do save.

As importantly, when those who do save significant amounts leave their jobs, the majority choose to rollover the account as a lump sum instead of converting it to a pension annuity. This presents the individual with a whole new set of challenges. Managing the account to achieve long-term sustainability so that they don't eventually run out of money as well as producing current income requires an expertise that most people simply don't have. We'll discuss some strategies to consider in later chapters.

[2] EBRI Issue Brief No. 304, April 2007

This trend by employers to transfer retirement security responsibility from the employer to the employee also eliminates one of the greatest safeguards of traditional pensions - shared risk. We know that a certain percentage of us are not going to reach the "average" life expectancy age. Based on that knowledge, traditional pension annuities can provide a greater benefit for those who do survive by utilizing the assets of those who pass away prematurely. For most people the idea of leaving money on the table due to premature death is so distasteful it becomes the primary motivator for electing a lump sum rollover. When that rollover is elected however, they lose the opportunity to create a guaranteed income for life that is likely greater than what they can produce by investing the assets on their own.

Personal Savings

The third leg of the traditional retirement income security stool is our own personal savings and investments. Unfortunately, the savings rate in the U.S. has historically been dismal. Prior to the economic recession of 2008, the savings rate in the U.S. was a *negative* 1.5%. We were actually spending more than we earned. One silver lining of that economic crisis is that within just six short months, the personal savings rate jumped to over 6% of income. The questions however, are twofold. Is it too little too late? And will this increased savings trend continue once the crisis has passed?

In terms of saving for retirement, many people view their contributions to their employer-sponsored 401(k) as fulfilling their personal savings obligation for this third leg of the stool. What most fail to realize is that those contributions are really replacing their employer's contribution. According to the U.S. Bureau of Labor Statistics, 43% of U.S. households do not even have a retirement savings account. Of those that do, the average amount is less than $50,000. Even more shocking, the median amount in those retirement accounts is only $2,000, meaning that for half of the 57% of households that have a retirement savings account, the amount in that account is $2,000 or less. Combine these figures, and you come up with over 70% of US households having less than $2,000 saved for retirement.

While the numbers are grim for Baby Boomers of all ages, second-half boomers, now becoming known as "Generation Jones" are facing a particularly tight situation. Raised as the little brothers and little sisters of the leading-edge boomers, these now middle-aged adults have bought into the same promises and followed the same path as their elder boomer siblings in expectation of the same retirement payoff. But like a child arriving late to a party, Generation Jones is likely to find the cake and ice cream already gone.

The Splitting of a Generation

Contrary to popular belief, the Baby Boomers are not a single generation. Typically described as the 76 million Americans born between 1946 and 1964, the formative experiences of first half boomers were very different than those of second-half boomers. Whereas first-half boomers witnessed JFK's assassination and experienced Woodstock and the Vietnam War firsthand, second-half boomers were just children at the time. Their perceptions of the world were shaped by Watergate, disco, and the Iran hostage crisis. By the time the 1980s rolled around, first-half boomers were well into the accumulation phase of their lives (remember Michael Douglas's portrayal of Gordon "Greed is Good" Gekko from the 1987 movie *Wall Street*?) while second-half boomers were just graduating from college and beginning their careers.

This 18-year difference between the first boomers born in 1946 and last boomers born in 1964 has also translated into very different economic experiences. Whereas first-half boomers benefitted from the high interest rates of the early 1980s when CD rates were at 13%, they also suffered through inflation and mortgages of 14% as they were buying their first homes during the same time period. For second-half boomers who were still in school, this most recent great rise in U.S interest rates was a non-event.

As the economy stabilized in the 1980s and 90s the United States went on an unprecedented economic bull run, creating massive amounts of wealth. From January 2, 1980 to December 31, 1999, the Dow Jones Industrial Average soared from 824.57 to

11,497.12[3], an almost 1400% increase! Housing prices quadrupled from an average of $72,400 in 1980 to a peak of $329,400 in March of 2007[4]. Adding to the economic good times was the fact that inflation was held in check during that time at a relatively modest average rate of less than 3.5%.[5]

While economists attributed this increased wealth across the board to all Baby Boomers, clearly the first-half boomers born from 1946 to the early-1950s saw the greatest advantage. These leading-edge boomers were at a stage in their lives when they had already purchased a home or begun accumulating financial assets that could benefit from these rising values. Second-half boomers, who reached these life-stage milestones 10-15 years later ended up paying higher prices as their fellow boomers increased demand for those very same assets. Therefore, while leading-edge boomers were able to purchase assets at the bottom and ride them all the way to the top, second-half boomers were only able to get in well after prices had already begun to rise, and saw only a fraction of the gains that leading-edge boomers experienced.

To understand the difference in impact between the leading-edge Boomers and Generation Jones, let me pose a simple question. Would you rather receive $1 million dollars today, or receive a penny today and allow me to double the amount I give you every day for 30 days? Most of us would probably take the $1 million today. But if you did, as you can see in Table 3.1 on the next page, you'd be giving up over $4 million dollars!

[3] http://www.nyse.tv/dow-jones-industrial-average-history-djia.htm

[4] http://www.census.gov/const/uspricemon.pdf

[5] http://inflationdata.com

Day	Dollar Amount	Day	Dollar Amount
1	$ 0.01	16	$ 327.68
2	$ 0.02	17	$ 655.36
3	$ 0.04	18	$ 1,310.72
4	$ 0.08	19	$ 2,621.44
5	$ 0.16	20	$ 5,242.88
6	$ 0.32	21	$ 10,485.76
7	$ 0.64	22	$ 20,971.52
8	$ 1.28	23	$ 41,943.04
9	$ 2.56	24	$ 83,886.08
10	$ 5.12	25	$ 167,772.16
11	$ 10.24	26	$ 335,544.32
12	$ 20.48	27	$ 671,088.64
13	$ 40.96	28	$ 1,342,177.28
14	$ 81.92	29	$ 2,684,354.56
15	$ 163.84	30	$ 5,368,709.12

Table 3.1
One Penny Doubled Every Day for 30 Days

Now none of us are going to get too excited about turning one cent into two cents, or even $5 into $10. But when we start turning $10,000 into $20,000, $20,000 into $40,000 or $1 million into $2 million, now you've got my attention! The key is that you've got to get through those first few doubles that don't really look all that exciting before you can start talking about significant money.

For leading boomers who were able to enter the markets in the early 1980s when the Dow was in the 800s, they were able to get some of those smaller, less exciting doubles out of the way. By 1990 when the Dow had risen to 2810, that represented a 340% gain in just 10 years. A $1000 investment in 1980 would have grown to approximately $3,400 by 1990. Over the next 10 years as the Dow advanced from 2810 to 11,497 in late 1999, that $3,400 would have continued to grow to approximately $13,900. That's a slightly better than 400% return for the decade, but a whopping 1400% return for the two decades combined!

For Generation Jones, who were only beginning to establish themselves and may have started investing around 1990, their $1,000 investment actually did a little better than the leading boomers did in the 1980s as it grew to a little over $4,000. The problem for Generation Jones and for any leading-edge boomers who started investing later is that they didn't get the next decade worth of doubles. As the dot-com and technology bubbles burst in the early 2000s, then housing prices and the broader markets declined in the late 2000s, both Generation Jones and leading-edge Boomers have seen their asset values fluctuate wildly, but in the end remain relatively unchanged from where they were at the beginning of the decade. For leading-edge boomers who were able to get in early, that level is three times higher than it is for those who were delayed.

Certainly this isn't anyone's fault. Some in Generation Jones have complained for years of perceived economic "hand-me downs" from their early boomer siblings, but first-half boomers can't be blamed for the rising asset values of the 80s and 90s or economic turmoil of the past decade any more than any other generation. We have all contributed in both positive and negative ways. Further, an argument can be made that Generation Jones will have that much more time to allow their investments to make up the lost growth of the last decade, whereas leading-edge boomers are now facing an imminent retirement. For those leading-edge boomers who didn't begin saving and investing early, they too will face serious challenges. Thankfully, a greater percentage (although still nowhere near 100%) of them will have access to an employer's pension and likely be grandfathered into existing Social Security benefits.

There is no doubt that both cohorts are facing challenges. But the fact remains that just like the formative experiences of their youth, the investment experience of second-half boomers has been significantly different than that of leading-edge boomers. Combined with the maturation of Social Security and decline of employer-sponsored pensions, the result is that the retirement reality that second-half boomers are about to inherit will be significantly different as well.

Chapter 4

Rethinking the Goal

To many of us, retirement has become the final goal of our working careers. Not because we want to retire in the traditional sense, but because of what retirement now represents - a time of freedom to do what we really want. But what is it we really want? While the specifics may be different for each of us, over the years four common themes have emerged.

Four Themes of Retirement

Freedom - Without a doubt, more than any other single concept, retirement today means freedom. Freedom from worry and anxiety about money, freedom to spend our time as we please, and freedom from the obligations and responsibilities that tend to weigh so many of us down. While most of us tend to equate retirement freedom strictly with financial freedom, true freedom in retirement and at any other stage in our lives is about much more than just money.

Balance - The second common theme surrounding our perception of retirement today is that we all want more balance in our lives. Almost universally my clients felt they spent too much time at work and not enough time with family or pursuing other interests. While some sources suggest as many as 60% of us are dissatisfied with our jobs, other studies indicate that for many of us, it's not so much that we dislike our jobs, we just spend too much time at them!

Considering the economic trends of the past decade, it's not hard to see why. As profit margins have shrunk and Wall Street pressures have increased, many companies have responded by cutting their workforces. While those who still have their jobs are grateful, they are also under tremendous pressure as workloads get redistributed. It's not at all uncommon for one individual to now be responsible for the workload that two or three people were previously managing.

That increased work load makes it very difficult to take time off. The reality is that much of the work we miss while we're away simply piles up and is waiting for us when we return. We end up making up our time off by putting in unpaid overtime to dig out from underneath the mass of paperwork and e-mails waiting for us when we get back! Additionally, the fear of being labeled as less than dedicated and therefore being placed next in line to be laid off, or passed over for the next promotion, causes many of us to take our vacation days very sparingly. While the average American receives two weeks of paid vacation per year, we actually take considerably less. According to Expedia.com, Americans forfeited over 436 million vacation days in 2009.

When we do take time away from the office, we often end up taking the office with us. Cell phones, e-mail and BlackBerry's make us instantly accessible almost anywhere on the globe. Over 80% of executives report contacting the office at least once per day while supposedly on vacation.

The interesting part of all this is that a long-term study done by the Organizational Psychology Program at Rutgers Graduate School of Applied and Professional Psychology showed that employees who work 10-12 hours per day are significantly less productive and efficient than employees who work 6-6.5 hours a day. Our culture has come to believe that dedication to the job is shown by putting in a large number of hours. Not only does this lead to being less productive, but it also leads to burnout, stress and various other health issues.

Trying to restore some semblance of balance to our lives, therefore, becomes one of the major factors driving our desire to retire. It's not necessarily that we don't want to work; we just want to do something *besides* work. Retirement becomes viewed as that time in our lives when we can ease back from the rat race and explore other facets of our lives.

Purpose - The third major theme surrounding the ideal retirement today is the desire to achieve a sense of purpose in life. As we discussed at length in Chapter 2, the unfortunate truth for many of us is that the sense of purpose that we may once have felt in our career has long since faded away. Today we view retirement as a time we can re-establish a sense of purpose in our lives.

Passion - The final theme I hear over and over from people hoping to retire soon is the desire to truly start living again. Before my brain tumor was discovered, I had become one of the "walking wounded," essentially sleepwalking through my days. The routine was the same every day - get up, go to work, come home, go to sleep. I was bored stiff - just like my clients. I had tried several things to try to bring some excitement into my life. I had gone bungee-jumping, paragliding, rock climbing and rappelling - all in an effort to bring some passion and adventure back into my life. For a while, those things worked. And while I still enjoy many of those activities, I found that for me, they don't provide the true sense of passion that comes from engaging in a truly fulfilling purpose.

But these four themes - freedom, balance, purpose and passion - are not purely the province of the retired. We all want these qualities in our lives. To achieve them we need to challenge the assumptions we've made about retirement and set a goal of incorporating these essential qualities earlier in our lives.

Achieve a Number, or a Life?

The fact is, many of us are not happy - perhaps even miserable - in our jobs. We look forward to retirement as both a way out of these jobs we don't like, and as a time when we can finally achieve freedom, balance purpose and passion by doing what we've always wanted to do. As we saw in the last chapter, however, achieving the retirement we envision is getting harder and harder to do.

When considering these three points collectively it's no wonder that retirement planning is the number one financial concern for the majority of leading-edge boomers and Generation Jones. Emerging out of this concern is a growing fixation on the "number" - how much money each of us will need to save to create the retirement we envision. Books, software programs, investment firms and financial services companies of all types attempt to provide us with tools that will help us determine our own personal number.

But in our quest to achieve our number, are we actually getting closer to the life we want to lead, or are we driving ourselves further away? Is our goal truly to accumulate a certain "number" or is it to create a passionate life? My client John was a perfect example of pursuing a number while forgetting about his life.

John was a highly paid executive at a large regional telecommunications firm. He had started his career as an electrical engineer and spent almost 15 years in research and development, designing and creating new products for his employer. As John told me, "That was the best time of my life. I loved creating new products and seeing my ideas come to life." Because he was so good at what he did, John received several promotions and went from being a team member to running the team, then running the department and eventually running the entire division.

Along with his career success, John also experienced financial success. His $250,000+ per year salary allowed him to pay off his million-dollar home in a prestigious neighborhood and a nice second "mountain home" in the Colorado Rockies. He had been able to accumulate approximately $6 million dollars in savings and investments and by all accounts - at least according to 99% of other Americans - had arrived at the good life.

The problem was that John's job had become extremely stressful. He developed stomach ulcers, high blood pressure and a variety of other physical ailments as a result of his long hours and high stress. He wanted out. He was tired of the endless meetings, bureaucratic red tape, political infighting and the constant pressure. He told me that his dream was to start a small company and get back to doing what he really loved to do – designing products. In fact, he had just been presented with the perfect opportunity. John had been approached by a doctor friend of his who had given him an idea for a new medical device that he felt he could develop for very little money. On the surface it seemed like everything was falling into place. Once again a client surprised me when his question to me was not "How can I make this happen?" but, "How quickly can you grow my $6 million dollar portfolio to $8 million dollars?"

Somewhat taken aback, I asked why he felt he needed $8 million dollars. Did he need more monthly income? No, the income we could safely generate off of the $6 million would be more than enough. Did he need start-up capital for his new business? No, that funding would come from other investors. Did he have other goals or other large personal expenses he anticipated at some point in the future? No, in fact he was actually considering selling one of his houses.

Puzzled, I finally asked, "Help me understand why you feel you need this additional $2 million dollars?"

To which he calmly replied, "It's the number I've set as my goal. It's what I need before I'll feel comfortable making a move."

John was clearly financially independent, but just as clearly he was not financially free. John suffered from the same affliction that I had at one time - the accumulation addiction - the feeling that no matter how much he had saved it was never enough. Even after I showed him several scenario projections indicating that his current savings and investments were more than enough to meet his needs, he was still convinced that he needed to achieve his "number" before he would feel secure enough to make a move. His belief that he needed "just a little bit more" was so powerful that even in the face of declining health and logical proof that he had saved "enough," he chose to delay making changes that would greatly improve his quality of life.

Financial Freedom vs. Independence

For years we have used the terms financial independence and financial freedom interchangeably to describe a financial state of "enough." If people were financially independent they were automatically assumed to also be financially free. But financial freedom is not just about having a lot of money. Our world is littered with examples of mismanaged wealth. According to the

National Basketball Association's Player's Association, 60% of retired NBA players go broke within five years of leaving the NBA. Sports Illustrated reports that almost 80% of National Football League players are flirting with bankruptcy within two years of leaving the NFL, and stories of celebrity bankruptcies are common. It's even estimated that approximately one-third of lottery winners are bankrupt within five years of their winning day. If simply having a lot of money led to financial freedom, why are so many multimillionaires going broke?

Over the years I have come to realize that there is indeed a significant difference between financial independence and financial freedom. Financial independence is a mathematical equation; a logical, tangible, provable calculation based on the amount of income needed compared to the amount of assets accumulated. Financial freedom on the other hand, is an intangible emotion.

While John was financially independent - meaning that if he managed his wealth properly, he would never have to work again - he was not financially free. John was still worried whether he had "enough," and as a result did not feel the freedom or security necessary to make the changes he so desperately wanted to make. His fear that he would not have enough created an insecurity that tied him to his job.

When I asked my clients what financial freedom meant to them, they often said it was simply being free from the worry, stress and anxiety that money causes in our lives. Most of us tend to assume that equates to having a lot of money so we don't have to worry about how we're going to pay the bills and afford all the things we want to do. As we saw with John however, having a lot of money doesn't necessarily free you from that worry and anxiety. Those who have a lot of money often suffer the same level of stress around money as those who struggle to make ends meet. What they worry about is slightly different, but the worry is still there.

And while it is possible, like John, to be financially independent but not financially free, it's also possible to be financially free but not financially independent. My client Emma was good example of that.

Emma was a 48 year-old single mother of two who worked as a secretary in a small law firm. Emma's husband, Tom, had passed away four years earlier when her children were 9 and 11 years old. While the life insurance settlement she received was helpful, Emma was by no means financially independent.

For years, Emma had harbored the dream of one day opening a small artist's boutique. She herself had dabbled in painting and knew several other amateur artists in the area who needed an outlet for their creations. Before Tom died, the two of them had talked often about opening a small store where local artists could display and sell their work. After Tom's passing, it looked as if that dream would never be realized.

But after a couple of years, after the shock of Tom's passing had worn just a tiny bit away and once Emma and the kids had gotten back into a routine, the old dream began to nudge at her again. A feeling of restlessness came over her as she felt compelled to pursue her dream.

While she generally enjoyed her job and the people she worked with, it just wasn't fulfilling. "I'd push paper and file motions on divorce cases all day," she once told me. "I'd see these couples in bitter battles and think to myself 'Do they really have any notion of what they're throwing away?' I'd give anything just to have another day with Tom."

Eventually the negativity of the environment got to her. "I got to a point where I couldn't see myself staying there until I retired. I mean, what's the point? The people I worked with were all nice enough, but it was bringing me down. I kept asking myself what difference I was making."

Emma then took a bold move. "I confided in my boss what I was thinking about in opening a small store. I knew it was risky, but he had lots of experience and contacts. I hoped that by approaching him directly, we might be able to work something out."

Her move paid off. Emma's boss turned her on to a number of resources and classes where she learned about business planning, marketing and operating a small business. She also met other like-minded people who provided assistance and began to get the word out about what she was planning to do. "I had artists from all over the state calling to see if I would be willing to put their work in my shop. And this was before it even opened! My only fear was if I could get buyers into the shop."

Recognizing that cash flow was likely to be thin for a while, Emma increased her emergency savings and cut her personal expenses wherever possible. "Things were lean and mean around the house. We didn't spend much money and the kids didn't really like that. But I knew if I was going to pull this off we had to save and cut back as much as we could."

Finally the big day came. With her personal finances in order and a new lease on a Main Street storefront, Emma left her job and opened her boutique. "It was stressful. You never know how something like that is going to work out. People tell you you'll be successful and that they love your stuff, but you never know if they'll actually open their wallets."

After a successful grand opening, things slowed down and eventually returned to a sustainable pace. "It wasn't easy, but I'm glad I did it. My whole life has changed. Instead of being stuck in that office I now get to be around people who share the same passions I do. The money is still sometimes an issue, but now I know what we can do to cut back and make it through the lean times."

Emma is still not financially independent, but she is free of the accumulation addiction that binds so many of us to the jobs and/or lives that we want to leave behind. She's learned how to budget, prioritize and generally manage her finances in a way that has allowed her to create the life she wants. By clearly focusing on her priorities and then exercising the discipline to make it happen, Emma was able to free herself from a job she didn't like and then create the life she wanted. In that respect, Emma is indeed financially free.

Both John's and Emma's stories have important lessons to teach us about the accumulation addiction. The first is about clearly identifying and sticking to our priorities. Motivational speaker Zig Ziglar was among the first to point out how most of us misplace the priorities of Have, Do and Be. Like John, most of us seek to find happiness in the things we have. The traditional thinking says that if we *have* enough of something we can *do* the things we want to do and we will finally *be* happy. The misplaced order of Have, Do and Be lie at the heart of the accumulation addiction. We mistakenly believe that if we can just accumulate or *have* enough, we will finally *be* happy. True satisfaction, according to Ziglar and demonstrated by Emma, comes from *Being* the kind of person who *Does* the things he or she needs to do. It is in the *Doing* of those things that we will find, create, and *Have* the happiness and satisfaction we all seek. It is in the being and doing that happiness is created.

Second, we need to recognize that we each have more than just financial resources available to create our ideal lives. We also have our personal human resources, or "human capital." While this notion is definitely changing, too many of us continue to cling to the idea that retirement means no longer earning a significant income. We don't worry about developing our human capital because we mistakenly believe that retirement means we won't have to use it. Our goal is to be financially independent, and therefore we shouldn't have to work or apply our skills.

But as many early retirees tell us and we'll see later in this book, a life of pure leisure and recreation quickly becomes boring and monotonous. We each need a purpose in our lives. We need something that makes us feel valued and appreciated. By applying our human capital – our unique combination of strengths, talents, skills and abilities that each of us are born with and subsequently develop through education and experience – we can make a difference that provides meaning and satisfaction to our lives. By *being* the type of people who develop their human capital, we can then *do* the things we want and subsequently *have* the life we truly want. When we apply our human capital to a specific, meaningful purpose, we can experience lasting happiness and contentment.

A New Goal

While Emma is certainly not the only person to ever leave a secure job in pursuit of a dream, she is among a small minority. As we saw with Ed in Chapter 2, the idea of making as much money as we can in hopes of reaching the retirement finish line as quickly as possible is still the primary goal for most of us. But that goal is slowly changing.

As early as 2001, William D. Novelli, then Executive Director and CEO of AARP suggested that earned income will be a critical element in securing one's retirement. With the crumbling pillars of corporate pensions, Social Security and lack of our own personal savings, it's not hard to see he may well be right. But does that mean we have to wait even longer to create the lives we want? Fortunately, the answer is no. To achieve that life however, we need to start looking differently at how our lives are "supposed" to go.

In 2005, J Peter Lindquist, author of the book *Solving the Retirement Puzzle,* was among the first to suggest that the three life stages around which we've built our lives and our culture no longer fit the realities of how we live today. He suggested that a new life stage is emerging between career and retirement that satisfies both our financial need to earn an income and our emotional need to self-actualize. Calling this new life stage "Pretirement," Lindquist suggested this new four life-stage model, will eventually become the new "normal" life stage progression.

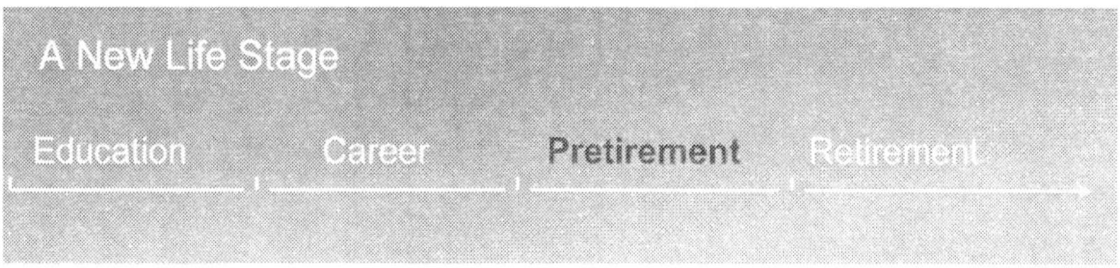

Trends Driving Pretirement

As we look at what's happening in our culture today, we see three trends that are driving the emergence of pretirement as a new life stage.

The first trend is the increased amount of time we'll likely spend in retirement. This increased time is due to:

- Our increased life expectancies and better health as we age, and
- A decline in the average retirement age (as compared to 50 years ago.)

In 1950 the average worker left the workforce at age 68 and was expected to live to be 77 years old, meaning they would spend

9 years or roughly 12% of their lives in retirement. By 2005, the average American left the workforce at age 62 and is now expected to live to be 83, meaning they could spend 21 years or 25% of their lives in retirement. (For decades from the 1950s to the 1990s the average retirement age in the U.S. steadily declined until around 2000 when it began to climb, but is still lower today than it was in 1950.) For those who retire early, say at age 55, they can expect to spend a full 1/3 of their lives in retirement.

The second trend driving this new life stage is our collective, cultural desire to self-actualize. People want to give back, to make a difference and find meaning in their lives. They want to engage in something that provides a strong sense of purpose and fulfillment.

The trend toward self-actualization is also driven by two factors. The first is simply the advancement of our culture which allows us to more easily meet our basic physiological and safety needs and therefore more quickly ascend Maslow's hierarchy. We don't need to know how to grow our own food or build our own shelters, we simply need to know how to manage our money so we can acquire the food and other things we need to survive. (Effective money management has replaced many of these ancient skills as one of today's most basic survival skills. We'll begin covering that in Chapter 8.)

The second factor driving this collective, cultural trend to self-actualize is demographics. When the boomers were attempting to meet their esteem needs in the 1980s, 90s and early 2000s, they were in a highly consumptive phase of their lives. Now that the boomers have reached the self-actualization stage, we have a significant and sizable portion of the population collectively creating a cultural change.

The third trend driving the creation of this new life stage of pretirement is the financial need of individuals to continue to earn an income. With the financial challenges of supporting a 20-30 year retirement as described in Chapter 3, coupled with the desire to give back and find ways to make a meaningful contribution, many workers in their 40s, 50s and 60s are re-training and re-tooling themselves to continue to earn an income doing something they truly enjoy, with the intention of doing it for as long as they can.

For someone who loves what they do, retirement is no longer a goal, but neither is the work-till-you-drop-just-to-get-ahead mentality that drives us early in our careers. As a life stage, pretirement allows us to do what we naturally and instinctively want to do. When we reach middle age, we each have a natural inclination to review how we've lived our lives up to that point, and re-assess how we want to live the second half of our lives. Our priorities change. Instead of being driven by power, wealth, status and achievement, we're now driven by a desire to simplify, to achieve balance in our lives and to make a difference in the world.

By adding a new life stage - call it whatever you want - we break free of the myth-assumptions that prevent us from achieving the life we want. When the goal of retirement and the idea that we need to accumulate a small fortune to get there is removed, there's no longer anything preventing us from creating the life we want today. We no longer have to retire first before we can do what we've always wanted. When we recognize and accept that we can earn an income by doing something we truly enjoy, we free ourselves of the accumulation addiction that traps us in jobs we've grown tired and bored with. When we recognize that what we're "supposed" to do is to be happy with the journey of life, not just the destination of retirement, we allow ourselves the freedom to make changes that will improve our lives today, without worrying about how they'll affect our retirement tomorrow.

Here, I believe, is the key. People don't want to retire, we want to be happy. Unfortunately, we've come to believe that retirement equals happiness. We've morphed the concept of retirement to encompass whatever our ideal life vision happens to be, even though for most of us the details are ill-defined and sketchy at best. We view retirement as a way out of a situation that we've grown tired of, and bestowed upon it an ideal that few are able to achieve. With the financial challenges that retirement represents, the traditional three life-stage model is setting many of us up for major disappointment in the latter half of our lives. The idea that there is a fourth life stage that fits between career and retirement allows us to change the goal that drives so much of our lives. Instead of being driven to reach some artificial retirement finish line, we can focus on creating happiness, contentment and fulfillment today. Pretirement allows us to create the lives we want today and relieves the pressure and stress of preparing for "retirement."

Chapter 5

A New Set of Beliefs

To achieve the freedom, balance, purpose and passion we all seek, not only do we have to overcome the myth-assumptions of retirement, but we also need to replace those assumptions with a new set of beliefs. Three beliefs that are critical to creating the life you want today are:

1. Work is not the enemy, but meaningless work is.
2. Effectively managing our financial resources creates freedom.
3. Happiness and fulfillment come from balancing Six Key Life Arenas.

Work Is Not the Enemy, but Meaningless Work Is

It's been said that if you truly love what you do, you'll never work another day in your life. To illustrate this first point, we need look no further than my client Betty.

Betty is a care coordinator for a major health insurance company. Her job is to meet with people who are homebound to make sure they are getting the care they need to recover from major medical procedures or conditions. Betty is perfect for the job. She's bright, happy, optimistic, enthusiastic and cares deeply for the people she serves. And at 74, she's both older and more energetic than most of the people she works with.

As Betty's financial advisor, I knew that financially she was well capable of retiring and being able to do whatever she wanted to do. One day, after reviewing her portfolio I asked her if she had given any thought to our earlier conversations of retirement. She said, "You know, I have. And what I've decided is that if I could do anything at all, I would do exactly what I'm doing now. I love the people I work with. I stay active and involved in the community. I take time off to travel when I want to, and when I get home I know I have something to go back to. And more than anything, I know that I make a difference in people's lives. It feels good. Truthfully, I don't want to retire. I'm going to continue to do this as long as they'll let me."

The reality is, work is not the enemy, but meaningless work is. We all want to be useful and productive, and feel as though our contributions make a difference. It's only when we lose that sense of fulfillment from our jobs do we begin to look at retirement as a way out. But if, like Betty, we can find work that is meaningful and fulfilling, there's no reason to leave.

Effectively Managing Our Financial Resources Creates Freedom

The second belief we need to adopt is that financial freedom doesn't come from having large amounts of money, but from effectively managing the money that we do have. I learned this lesson from a couple that surprised me more than any client ever has.

Early in my career, I met with a couple named Tom and Sue. Tom worked as a line repairman for the local telephone company, while Sue was a stay-at-home mom raising their six children. Now with their youngest about to head off to college and both of them in their early 50s, they had come to see me to talk about retirement planning.

As we talked, I became very impressed with their financial situation. Tom earned an average wage at the time - around $45,000 a year. And while they had never received an inheritance or any other wealth windfall, they had no debts, owned their home free and clear, and even after putting all six children through private school and helping them with college, they had a nice retirement nest egg of almost $400,000. Assuming Tom would retire around age 60, it looked like there was plenty of time to grow that nest egg even more. But just to confirm, I asked, "So, when would you like to retire?"

"I've already submitted my paperwork," Tom said. "I'm done at the end of the month."

Now, from a financial planning perspective, retiring before age 59 1/2 creates some special challenges, but considering how well prepared they were, I sensed there must be more to the story. "Okay," I said, "What's the plan?"

"We're going on a mission for our church," Sue explained. "For two years - to Lithuania. After that, we plan on doing another somewhere in Africa. Since our housing will be paid for, we just need to cover food, clothing and incidentals."

"How much do you think you'll need for that?" I asked.

"About $10,000 a year," Tom replied.

"I've got to tell you," I said. "I'm very impressed. There aren't too many folks these days who can raise six children in a one-income household and still save enough to retire early. How'd you do it?"

"Two things," Sue said. "We're very clear about our goals and what's important to us, and we only spend money on those things. When we bring Coke into the house the kids think it's a treat."

Now I'm not sure we all want to budget our spending to that degree, but the point is well-made. Most of us have neither the well-defined goals nor the discipline to pull off what Tom and Sue were able to do. But for those who do, the payoffs are tremendous.

Balance the Six Key Life Arenas

The third truth is that happiness and fulfillment come from balancing and fulfilling Six Key Life Arenas. Scientists have shown that 99.9% of all human DNA is the same within each of us, with only one-tenth of 1% accounting for all of our differences in gender, race, hair and eye color and all the other differences that make each of us unique. While the details of our lives are as different as our fingerprints, the core elements that create happiness and fulfillment are as universal as our DNA. At our core, each of us wants for ourselves and our loved ones to be happy, safe, prosperous and fulfilled. Unfortunately the threats that often prevent us from achieving that dream can come from a variety of areas in our lives.

In 2008 the web site Boomertowne.com conducted an informal survey by asking one simple question, "Are you generally happy with your life?" Out of more than 121,000 responses an overwhelming majority – 92% - responded no, they were generally not happy with their lives. How is it that we can live in the wealthiest nation on earth, with more opportunity and freedoms than any people have ever known, and yet so many of us are still unsatisfied with our lives?

Over the past decade extensive research has been done in an attempt to determine just what it takes to be happy, content and fulfilled. Assuming that our basic physiological and safety needs as defined by Maslow are consistently met, the higher-level needs all tend to revolve around six different "life arenas" within which all the other variables in our lives will fall. Success in balancing and fulfilling each of these Six Key Life Arenas generally leads to happiness and a high quality of life. While some may categorize or title them slightly differently, these are the keys that I've seen emerge time and time again.

1. Engage in a fulfilling purpose

2. Practice Financial Maturity

3. Continue personal growth and development (including spirituality)

4. Connect with family and friends

5. Maintain health and wellness

6. Develop leisure and lifestyle interests

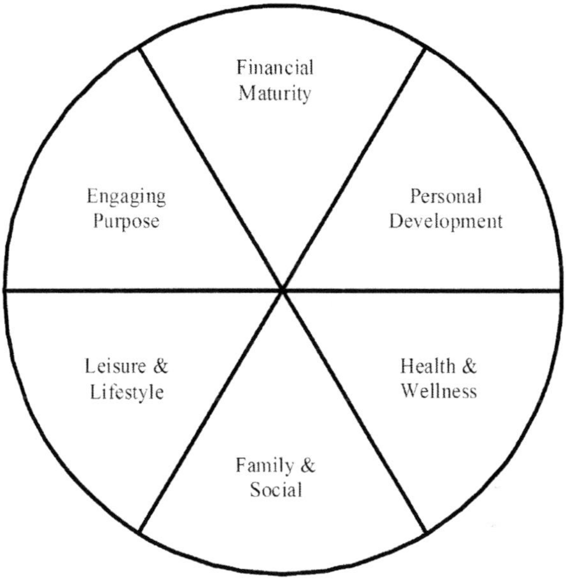

Figure 5.1
The Six Key Life Arenas

You may be surprised to notice that career and work are not among the six arenas. That's because my observation of some of my more successfully retired and happiest non-retired clients has shown that while a job may support several of the six arenas, it is not a requirement by itself. Many people do indeed find a sense of purpose, mental stimulation, a sense of identity and opportunities for personal growth among other benefits within their work. Yet many others find all those things without holding a formal job. If one has achieved both financial independence and financial freedom they may still (and often do) choose to continue to work to fulfill these other, emotional needs, or they may find that fulfillment from their hobbies, volunteering or any number of other activities. Conversely, if our personal financial situation dictates that we do need to continue to earn an income, finding work that you love and that fills many of these arenas will leave you more energized and engaged in all areas of your life.

Engage in a Fulfilling Purpose

Regardless of whether you are currently working, retired, or even unemployed, engaging in a fulfilling purpose is key to a happy and successful life. Having something personally meaningful that you can apply your energies toward is essential to building feelings of self-esteem and self-worth.

When we talk about purpose however, it's important to recognize that it does not have to be some great, philosophical ideal. I know many people are intimidated by the prospect of setting out on a journey to discover their "Life Purpose." (Imagine big booming, echoing sound effects when you read those two words.) Let's face it, if in fact each of us has only one true life purpose, and we were to discover that we either couldn't find it, or couldn't live it, that would be fairly depressing.

The reality is that each of us has several "purposes" in our lives. Some may hit closer to our hearts than others, but all can provide a sense of fulfillment and satisfaction. The only requirement is that whatever it is you choose needs to be completely engaging of your heart, your mind and your soul. If finding a cure for cancer is what your heart calls you to do, then by all means pursue it. But oftentimes the smallest gesture fulfills the largest purpose. Taking meals to the homebound, caring for an aging or dependent family member, or being a mentor to someone in need are all simple expressions of a profound purpose. However you choose to express your purpose, the only requirement is that your purpose be meaningful to you. English poet William Cowper once said, "The only true happiness comes from squandering ourselves for a purpose." Fulfilling that purpose helps to define the value of our contribution to others and adds worth and meaning to our lives.

Practice Financial Maturity

Earlier we talked about the difference between financial independence and financial freedom, but to achieve both we must first be Financially Mature.

Financial Maturity involves four key elements. The first is the need to have a healthy relationship with money. Virtually every major decision we make involves some consideration of the monetary consequences. What we do, where we live and who we associate with are all impacted by our attitudes and beliefs about money. Often, those attitudes and beliefs come from childhood or cultural experiences that taint our perspective. Examining the source of our attitudes and beliefs allows us to discard those that no longer serve our purpose. This perspective then allows us to create a new set of attitudes and beliefs that are truly aligned with our values. By aligning our attitudes, beliefs and actions around money with our personal values and purpose, we create a healthy perspective that eliminates much of the stress and turmoil that money can create in our lives.

Second, we need to educate ourselves in the areas of personal finance. Having a working knowledge of our personal financial statements, assets, debts, income and expenses, tax rules and the impact each has on the other is critical. You do not need to become an investment expert, but you should understand basic investment concepts. If you are considering giving up your current income stream by retiring or changing jobs, you should also understand basic income distribution strategies. We'll start covering the financial information you need to know in Chapter 8.

Third, you need to prepare yourself in two ways. You need to save and accumulate assets, but you also, and perhaps more importantly, need to get a very firm understanding of your total expenses that are required to support your lifestyle. How much is "enough" to save and accumulate for financial independence is directly dependent on how much you spend. Likewise, if you are not ready for retirement but would like to consider a job or career change, knowledge of your expenses and potential income from your accumulated assets is critical to developing an earnings strategy that will allow you to make that change.

The final element of Financial Maturity is to exercise the discipline to stick to your plan. For many, this has a negative connotation that feels restrictive or limiting. But for the Financially Mature, that discipline represents the freedom to spend our time as we choose and the peace of mind that comes from having a strong handle on our finances. Just as our social freedom depends on rules of law that serve a greater purpose (the safety and security of everyone,) so too does our financial freedom. For the Financially Mature, the discipline to live within their means supports the greater purpose of creating the freedom to spend their days pursuing the activities they choose. That same discipline also provides peace of mind and confidence in our financial security.

Continue Personal Growth and Development

Psychologists have long recognized that to fully develop as individuals, each of us will go through two broad life transformations. The first involves creating identities as we transition from adolescence to adulthood. This phase involves differentiation of skills and abilities so we can find our place in the world. A second transformation occurs, for some as early as our mid-30s but typically in our 40s or 50s, as we begin to question the completeness of our lives. As we enter or progress through this phase, the challenge of re-discovering who we are, what we're passionate about and redefining who we want to become takes on new importance.

For many, we've "become" our jobs. We describe ourselves as accountants, lawyers, engineers, managers or something similar. Our very identity is often tied up in what we do, and for many that's no longer enough. It's not unusual to use this time as a period of reflection to evaluate how we've lived our lives up to this point, and confirm a new or existing direction for how we'll live the second half of our lives.

While some have a very clear idea of what this direction will be, others will need to go through a process of self-discovery. Clearly identifying your values, personal and spiritual beliefs, motivators and priorities are all essential to figuring out who you are and achieving an inner sense of peace. Many will use this time to embark on an inner spiritual journey to discover their life purpose, while others will be content to develop character traits they feel are lacking.

Connect with Family and Friends

Perhaps the most important of the six arenas, maintaining and deepening your relationships with the people whom you value most is key to a happy life. Often the relationships we value most are the very ones we sacrifice in pursuit of our career and financial goals. As I experienced firsthand, it's the desire to renew and strengthen those relationships that often becomes the primary motivator for seeking change in our lives.

Transitioning careers or from career to retirement can by itself cause significant stresses on those relationships. While the goal is to strengthen the relationship, a sudden change in the schedule of one spouse often has a huge impact on the other. Two anecdotal studies are often cited that indicate the desire to spend more time with family is a contributing factor in over 75% of retiree's decisions to retire, while over 79% of retired couples report the additional time spent with one another is a cause of stress in the relationship! That's why the other arenas - engaging in a fulfilling purpose, continued personal growth and development and developing leisure and lifestyle interests - are so important. They help to ensure that we are emotionally healthy enough as individuals so that we don't become dependent on our significant others to fulfill all of our personal needs.

Beyond our spousal or other committed relationships however, many of us will look to strengthen relationships with our children, parents and siblings. We'll find time to re-connect with friends we've long neglected, and seek to create new friendships with others who share our newfound interests.

Unfortunately, many who have devoted themselves to their careers find the majority of their social relationships are work-related. When retiring or changing jobs, they often find those friendships no longer have the common ground to keep them active. Staying engaged socially by getting involved in community activities with others who share your interests will help to maintain healthy social relationships.

Maintain Health and Wellness

It's another of life's great oddities that with as much as we know about the importance of diet, exercise and mental stimulation, so many of us continue to pursue lifestyles that are detrimental to our overall well-being. While the process of aging can't be stopped, it's important to realize it is not a linear process. Its pace advances in sudden starts and stops, with periods of relative stability followed by periods of rapid or gradual decline, much of which we can influence.

While genetic factors do impact both our physical and mental abilities as we age, new studies are continually confirming that our lifestyle choices do indeed significantly contribute to the *pace* at which we age. In their book *Successful Aging*, authors John Rowe, M.D and Robert Kahn, PhD, illustrate that the effects of genetics shrink proportionately as we age, while lifestyle choices play an increasingly larger role in both our physical and mental aging. Obviously there are no guarantees, but evidence now incontrovertibly shows we can increase our odds of extended physical health and mental acuity by exercising both our bodies and our minds.

Just as the other arenas are inter-related, maintaining physical health and mental wellness will also contribute to your success in the other arenas. Maintaining your physical and mental capacity will allow you to pursue work you love, which in turn contributes to your economic wellness, sense of purpose and personal growth and development.

Develop Leisure and Lifestyle Interests

Perhaps the most fun of the six arenas, developing our leisure and lifestyle interests provides the opportunity to add more pure joy and contentment to our lives. Whether it's developing a personal interest or skill within yourself or participating in new activities with a group, pursuing the activities that are personally meaningful and enjoyable provide richness and color to our lives.

Especially when combined with family and friends, this is when we create the memories that stay with us forever.

To some however, the idea of leisure has become synonymous with rest, relaxation and the avoidance of anything strenuous. Unfortunately, our culture is filled with passive leisure options that consume our time but do little to engage our minds or bodies. While pleasant perhaps, these types of activities are rarely satisfying or meaningful.

To truly find joy in your hobbies requires you to get involved. You need to actively participate. Whether it is by yourself or with friends, your leisure activities should engross your mind and energize your body. Active leisure allows you to develop personal skills, express your creativity, build bonds with the people you care about and stretch your physical or mental abilities.

All the curve balls that can threaten our happiness in retirement or at any other time in our lives come from one of these Six Key Life Arenas. When one area is lacking, we typically tend to focus our attention in that area until we can resolve whatever shortcoming we may be experiencing. In the case of preparing for retirement, typically the focus is on accumulating enough money so we can *then* go pursue a fulfilling purpose. But even in cases where my clients have achieved their financial goal, they've done so at the expense of one or more of the other areas. I've seen clients so focused on wealth accumulation or advancing their careers that their marriages have ended in divorce, their health has failed, or they've completely forgotten how to simply have fun. The key to lasting happiness is to find balance and fulfillment within all six areas. Like a tire that hits a nail, it takes only one hole in one area of the tire to make the whole tire go flat and disrupt the journey.

Chapter 6

Defining Your Vision

So what does your ideal life look like? Would you be independently wealthy and traveling the world, or would you spend more time with friends and family? Would you take classes to pursue a new career, or would you volunteer with an organization that is personally meaningful to you? Regardless of your present situation, creating your ideal life involves two steps. First, you need to create a vision of exactly what that life looks like, and second, you need to define specific steps you can take to begin moving in that direction.

I have created two tools to help you create that vision and define those steps. The first is this book. This chapter is filled with exercises where you'll be asked to put pen to paper to create a written vision of your ideal life. The second tool is an online Life Planning Profile assessment that you can find at www.Retirement2020.com. The Life Planning Profile is a 90-question assessment covering the Six Key Life Arenas that produces a detailed report with specific action items based on your unique responses. You can access the Life Planning Profile free of charge by registering at www.Retirement2020.com/book10.

Defining your ideal life is no small task, but neither should it be a monstrous undertaking. We are all "works in progress" and therefore what we define as our ideal life will change over time. When I was a teenager I dreamt of being a professional athlete. Now in my mid-40s and only 5 feet 9 inches tall, I can safely say my childhood dream of playing quarterback in the NFL isn't going to happen. But that doesn't mean I can't enjoy and find satisfaction in playing various recreational sports now.

Creating a vision of your ideal life includes dreaming as big as you want to dream, and then testing that dream against the filter of your current reality. A friend of mine has long dreamt of being a professional musician, but now married with two beautiful daughters, he has no desire to spend the weeks on the road that life as a professional musician requires. Instead, he has found a regular monthly gig at a local club that allows him to express his musical interests and still be present for his family.

The key is to balance these competing priorities to create a life that is both passionate and fulfilling. The Six Key Life Arenas identified in the previous chapter provide both a good starting point and a good filter for defining what your ideal life looks like.

After creating your vision, the next step is to define specific steps that will begin to move you in that direction. For many of us, it is simply a matter of taking the blinders off and allowing ourselves permission to begin to move in the direction we want to go. Too often we feel restricted by what we're "supposed" to do with our lives. We fail to follow our hearts or dreams because we feel pressure to do what our spouses, parents, friends and co-workers expect us to do. Giving yourself permission to dream, and follow those dreams, is the first specific step you can take to begin moving in the direction of your ideal life.

Depending on what your ideal life looks like, the specific actions you take could be quite varied. It could include taking classes or going back to school. It might include starting a small business on the side or making a complete career change. It could mean consciously taking more time away from work and spending more time with friends and family. Whatever it is, it's likely to have financial consequences. Starting in the next chapter, we'll look at how arrange your finances in such a way as to allow you to pursue whatever your next steps may be.

Taking a Holistic View

Creating a vision of your ideal life requires looking at all Six Key Life Arenas, along with two additional areas that could impact those life arenas. The first additional item to look at is to identify your dreams. Each of us has dreams that we hold deep inside that we seldom let others see. Sometimes we withhold them from even our most significant relationships. But to truly create a life of purpose and passion, we need to look at those dreams and try to find a way, like my musician friend, to bring that dream alive in our lives.

The second additional item you'll look at is your job. Considering how much time most of us spend at work, our jobs often play a huge role in our lives that bleeds over to the other key life arenas. Many of us get a strong sense of identity, a sense of purpose and even the majority of our social interactions from our jobs. Understanding how that job impacts all areas of our lives is critical. More than once I've watched a client retire from a job they hated, only to discover there were many other lifestyle attributes associated with that job that they quickly came to miss.

In the following sections, we'll talk about five of the Six Key Life Arenas plus your dreams and your job. The Financial Maturity arena will be covered in detail in later chapters. I've provided a number of self-discovery exercises to both raise awareness of areas that might not be as fulfilling as you would like, and to begin provoking thoughts about what you can do to improve your satisfaction within each arena.

Examining Your Dreams

The first step in creating a vision of your ideal life is to identify your dreams. Don't worry about whether the dream is realistic or not, we'll pass it through the filter of reality later on. For now the goal is to simply dream as big as you can.

Many of us have one lifelong dream that immediately comes to mind. Others have several dreams, while still others have gotten so caught up in their day-to-day lives that they've forgotten the dreams of their youth. The following three questions have roots in both financial planning and in life/career coaching, and are intended to help you identify your deepest and most heartfelt dreams. Regardless of which group you fall into, take a moment to jot down answers to the following questions.

1. What would you do and how would you spend your time if you suddenly had all the money you would ever need? (Try to think beyond the immediate knee-jerk reactions of "quit my job" or "move to a warmer climate" and consider how you would spend your days after all those immediate wants are satisfied.)

____

____

____

____

____

2. What would you do if you knew you could not fail?

____

____

____

____

____

3. What regrets would you have if you suddenly discovered you were about to die?

____

____

____

____

____

At this point, one, two or maybe even three very heartfelt dreams should be beginning to take shape. Now we need to add some definition and clarity to each of those dreams. Take a moment to go to Appendix 1 at the end of this book and write out the particulars of your dreams in as much detail as possible.

Include the people you are with, the setting or environment you're in, what you are doing and what makes this dream so meaningful to you. What is it about this dream that really gets you excited? Do this for each of your dreams and feel free to use additional paper if necessary.

After you've written out each dream, go back and analyze each one. What is it that makes each dream great? Are there common themes that appear among all of them? Spend some time thinking about what makes each dream important to you. As we go through the remaining life arenas, look for ways where the important elements of your dreams can be tied into the other areas of your life.

Discover a Fulfilling Purpose

One of the biggest retirement lessons of the past decade has been that a life of complete leisure is really not much of a life at all. People need a purpose. We need something that engages us and allows us to contribute in a meaningful way to the larger world around us.

Discovering a purpose that we can feel committed to and provides a strong sense of satisfaction however, is sometimes both very difficult and very intimidating. Oftentimes when we talk about finding a sense of purpose we imagine some singular, grand, life-changing ideal. And while it is true that the closer to your heart you can come in defining and living out a personal purpose, the more satisfying it is likely to be, fretting over exactly what it will look like and settling for nothing less can also be very counterproductive. In an interview given to *Outside* magazine (May, 2009), Mike Rowe, host of the Discovery Channel program *Dirty Jobs,* says he certainly never dreamed of having a job that would require him to experience some of the filthiest working conditions imaginable. And yet as it turns out, *Dirty Jobs* is his ideal job. He's having more fun, impacting more people, and fulfilling a sense of purpose he never would have known had he been completely focused on following his heart (which, by the way, was to be an actor). Be open to what the world gives you. Watch for opportunities and be prepared to take advantage of those opportunities when they do arrive. Keep these four tips in mind as you search for your own opportunities.

1. Remember that your true purpose does not have to be some grand, world-changing ideal. As already mentioned, taking meals to the homebound, caring for an aging or dependent family member, or being a mentor to someone in need, are all simple expressions of a profound purpose. However you choose to express your purpose, the only requirement is that your purpose is meaningful to you.

2. Remember also that your purpose consists of two parts, both of which can be very broad and encompass a wide range of activities. According to Marcia Bench, founder of the Career Coach Institute, the first element of your purpose is known as the essence. The essence describes in very broad terms what you view as your true purpose - what it is you were born to do. For some people the essence can be as broad as saying "I want to help people." For most of us the essence of our purpose remains relatively stable and unchanging over time.

   The second element of your true purpose is in how you choose to express that purpose. What is it that you actually do to fulfill the essence of your purpose? Even here, a broader definition of how you choose to express that purpose provides more opportunities than smaller, narrower expressions. A purpose statement such as, "I want to help people improve their physical health," could be fulfilled by working in the medical profession, becoming a nutritionist or even as a personal trainer. A statement such as, "I want to help people improve their physical conditioning," has many fewer options. By not locking yourself into a narrow definition of how to express your purpose, you allow yourself the ability to make changes in your life without abandoning the essence of your purpose. Dr. Lloyd Thomas, co-author of *Total Life Coaching*, suggests that the essence of one's purpose should be intentionally as broad as it can be to allow more opportunities to express that purpose in a variety of ways.

3. Discovering your purpose is a process, not an event. There are dozens of tests and assessments out there that attempt to define your personality, identify your strengths and direct you to your true purpose. While some of these are very good and helpful, seldom is the answer revealed as the result of any single activity or event. Rather, the discovery of your true purpose is usually the result of several thought-provoking activities performed over a period of time with space in between to allow your sub-conscious mind time to mull-over what has been triggered during the exercises. Over time, certain themes begin to develop that instinctively feel as if you're heading down the right path. Sometimes those subconscious themes reveal themselves in a moment of "A-ha" clarity, while for others it will be just a gradual sense of growing confidence and commitment to a purpose that just feels right. The key is to allow yourself time to allow the answers to come to you.

4. Discovering your true purpose requires effort and self-examination. To get your subconscious mind to mull over the possibilities, you've got to consciously give it something to work on. This means setting aside time to dig into your memories, beliefs and values and ask yourself questions that you might prefer not to be asked. Make sure you set aside an appropriate amount of time in an environment free from noise and distraction to really focus on what you're trying to accomplish.

Now it's once again time to put pen to paper. Just like your dreams, you may already have a good sense of purpose. If so, you can skip the following exercises and proceed to the end of this section to write down your purpose. If not, the following exercises may help you discover a stronger sense of purpose.

1. Many times our most fulfilling sense of satisfaction comes from contributing to causes we feel passionately about. Take a moment to list below any causes that you feel strongly about. If you have trouble, try to remember back to a time when you felt especially moved by something. It may have been in the arts, a social injustice or an environmental cause. Whatever it was, it should stir deep emotions.

   Causes I Feel Strongly About:

____

____

____

____

2. Your true purpose will likely play off your strengths and natural gifts. While we're constantly told "You can be or do anything you want," the fact is we are all naturally gifted and inclined to do certain things better than others. Identifying your personal strengths and those things you do naturally well can provide critical clues to your true purpose. Note also that we're talking about strengths and gifts, not interests or activities. For an interest to graduate to a purpose, it should be something that you do naturally well. (If you're not sure what your strengths are, I've included a brief description of a variety of personality and strengths assessment programs at the end of this chapter to help you with further self-discovery.)

My Strengths:

____

____

____

____

3. Sometimes there are aspects of our present or past jobs that provide valuable clues as to our purpose. What about your present job do you thoroughly enjoy today? What has been your favorite job over your career? What was it about that job that you enjoyed?

Aspects of Past and Present Jobs I Have Enjoyed:

____

____

____

____

Just like with your dreams, it may be helpful to write stories about the causes, strengths and past/present aspects of your jobs that seem particularly fulfilling. Remember to add as much detail as possible to each story. What were you doing? Who were you with? Where were you? What was the challenge? How did you feel? Why did you feel that way? What made the experience enjoyable? Think like a reporter and try to answer the who, what, when, where, why and how of each situation with as much detail as you can remember.

When you have finished, look for common themes and try to put them into a purpose statement. Your purpose statement should express both what your purpose is and how you are going to fulfill it. For example, you might say, "My purpose is to help people improve their health by educating them on ways to achieve proper nutrition."

My purpose is to: ________________________________

by:_______________________________________

____

____

Continue Personal Growth and Development

Throughout our 40s and 50s it's only natural to spend some time reflecting on our lives up to this point. Our changing motivators, priorities and perspectives often cause us to make conscious changes in how we're going to live the rest of our lives. But making those changes is not always easy. Lifelong attitudes and beliefs must often be overcome and old habits can prove difficult to break. Those who have successfully transformed their lives site five key character traits as being essential to continued personal growth and development. These include self-understanding, self-acceptance, adaptability, optimism and a feeling of connection to something larger than themselves.

Self Understanding. For thousands of years various religions and philosophers have extolled the merit of self-understanding by teaching the directive of "know thyself" as the key to happiness and contentment. Today, there are any number of personality tests, psychological assessments and other tools available to help you figure out "who you are." In fact, we've included a short description of some of the more popular assessment tools at the end of this chapter.

While many of these tools are very helpful, the very best exercises are often the ones that force us to simply look inside ourselves just as we've done with the dreams and purpose story exercises in the previous sections. Deep within each of us, the theory goes, we all have a compass that continuously points toward our own true self. Over the years, that compass can become misaligned due to compromises, obligations and misplaced priorities. We often end up taking steps in directions away from our truest selves as we deal with the realities of day-to-day life.

By taking the time to undergo thoughtful introspection, we can re-calibrate that internal compass to ensure it points at our highest values and priorities. Many people find yoga, meditation, or simply the practice of sitting quietly for at least 15 minutes a day a good way to get in touch with those highest values. If you're a more hands-on type person, I've included a values exercise to help you identify your true values and priorities in Appendix 2.

Self-Acceptance. The human ego can be surprisingly fragile. Too often we beat ourselves up for the very characteristics that make us human. Whether they are perceived physical imperfections, mental capabilities or a shortage of desired skills, many of us tend to obsess over what we see as our shortcomings. To find true happiness, we need to learn to accept ourselves as we are. That doesn't mean we can't set goals for self-improvement, but our self-image and self-esteem should be based on the progress we make toward reaching those goals, not dependent solely on achieving a specific goal.

Adaptability. It's been said the only constant in the world is change. Not only do we change, but the world changes around us. Studies show that those who are more open and accepting of change tend to be happier and have a more positive outlook on life.

Optimism. Similarly, those who tend to view the glass as half-full instead of half-empty also tend to be happier. It's been suggested that optimism helps us see the opportunities that change often presents and give us hope for the future.

Connectedness. While spirituality is, of course, a personal choice, studies have shown that those who have a strong sense of spirituality tend to express a greater sense of inner peace. Whether it is a belief in God, a sense of "oneness" or "being," or a sense of connectivity to nature and the universe, fully connecting to something greater than ourselves can provide both strength and compassion when dealing with life's inevitable adversities.

To begin your own journey of personal growth, take a look at the following exercises.

1. Make a list of what you believe are the top five areas where you feel you need to grow. It may include developing those traits listed above, or it may be more specific traits such as becoming a better listener, developing greater patience or practicing greater empathy. Research and begin to practice ways to improve yourself in those areas.

   My Top Five Areas for Personal Growth:

____

____

____

____

____

2. Make a list of the top five priorities in your life, and then assess the amount of time and personal energy you expend toward those priorities. Many people find a great discrepancy between what they value and how they spend their time and energy. Aligning your efforts toward your values and priorities will provide for greater satisfaction and self-esteem.

   My Top Five Priorities in My Life:

____

____

____

____

____

Connect with Family and Friends

Perhaps the single greatest contributor to our happiness is the quality of our relationships with other people. In his book, *Solving the Retirement Puzzle*, J. Peter Lindquist very eloquently wrote, "Our relationships do more than save us from isolation; they bring us our greatest joys and greatest sorrows. They arouse all the emotions – love, pride, anxiety, anger, fear and happiness, among others – that make us human. Our relationships give meaning to our lives."

Now I am certainly not a relationship expert, but after consulting with various psychologists, life coaches and others I have discovered a few things any of us can do to improve the relationships in our lives.

The first step is to create a list of all the important people in your life. Organize that list by the three different types of relationships most of us have in our lives - our primary relationship with a spouse or significant other, family relationships with children, parents and siblings, and social relationships with friends. Your list might look something like this:

Family and Friends

Rate

My Primary Relationship: ____________________ _____

Family Relationships (Children, Parents, Siblings, Cousins, etc)

____ _____

____ _____

____ _____

____ _____

____ _____

____ _____

____ _____

Friends

____ _____

____ _____

____ _____

____ _____

____ _____

____ _____

____ _____

____ _____

The second step is to rate each relationship on a scale of 1-10 based on how satisfied you are with the relationship. You are NOT ranking the relationships in order of their importance to you, nor are you rating the people themselves. You are rating your own feelings of satisfaction about each relationship. Do you feel as close to that person as you would like? Do you spend enough time with them? Do you connect with them as deeply as you would like?

As you look at your list, several questions become obvious. Are there any glaring holes in your list? Are you satisfied with the number and depth of relationships you have? And are there any ratings that are significantly below where you would like them to be?

Just because a line is blank that does not mean there is a hole. Many people get along very well in life without a primary relationship. On the other hand, if you want but don't have a significant other in your life, you don't need this exercise to tell you that. No doubt you already know. What you can do however is recognize the abundance of other relationships in your life and strive to develop those to a fuller extent.

If you find that the number or depth of your relationships is less than you would like, consider joining clubs or other organizations of people who share your interests. The web site Meetup.com is a great place to find people and clubs in your area.

If you find there are some important people on your list where your ratings are significantly lower than you would like them to be, take a few moments to consider why. The reasons may be as varied as the people themselves but you might try the following exercise.

Take a moment to write a few paragraphs about each person on your list. What do you know about them? What are their likes and dislikes? Their strengths and weaknesses? What are the characteristics that both endear them to you or annoy you to death? What are their hopes and dreams? Their values and priorities? What are their struggles? Then, based on what you know about each person, consider what you can do to deepen each relationship. Are there things you don't know about them that perhaps you should? Are there things you can do to support their hopes and dreams or help them overcome their struggles?

Many years ago I ran across a quote about marriage that I think is equally applicable to any relationship we may have. It said,

"Having the perfect marriage is less about finding the perfect spouse than it is about being the perfect spouse." Whether it is with your spouse, children, parents or friends, look for things *you* can do to create deeper and more fulfilling relationships.

Maintain Health and Wellness

Like so many of us, prior to my brain tumor I had taken my health for granted. As I soon realized, no other aspect of our lives has the ability to change as suddenly or impact us more severely. Throughout our lives, how well we maintain our bodies and minds will largely determine our level of happiness, satisfaction and our ability to pursue fulfillment within each of the other key life arenas.

The good news is that much of our health is within our control. According to the World Health Organization, cardiovascular disease is responsible for half of all deaths in the United States. And yet, most of the major and contributing risk factors of cardiovascular disease are not genetic or environmental factors, but behavioral factors. High blood pressure, high cholesterol, physical inactivity, obesity, alcohol and tobacco use are all contributors, and are all controllable through our choices. By choosing to eat right, exercise and maintain a healthy weight, we can dramatically improve our odds of a long and physically healthy life.

Just as our bodies need nutrition and exercise, so too do our minds. According to the National Center for Health Statistics, Alzheimer's disease is now the sixth leading cause of death in the United States today. But for many, the fear of living with Alzheimer's is far greater than the fear of dying from it. Studies have shown that older individuals who continually challenge their minds, learn new things and even teach what they've learned to others, are less prone to Alzheimer's and tend to have a lower incidence of age-related mental disorders or decline. A life-long love of learning is one of the most useful traits to maintain mental acuity.

In the Life Planning Profile located online at Retirement2020.com, we ask ten simple questions related to health and wellness. Read through these questions to see if you're doing all you can to maintain your health and wellness.

	Yes	No
1. I'm in reasonably good health	☐	☐
2. I receive physical health checkups at least once per year	☐	☐
3. I exercise at least 3 times per week	☐	☐
4. I maintain my weight at recommended levels	☐	☐
5. I avoid excessive use of alcohol, tobacco & drugs	☐	☐
6. I enjoy reading thought-provoking articles and publications	☐	☐
7. I maintain my natural curiosity	☐	☐
8. I regularly stimulate and challenge my mind	☐	☐
9. I am rarely bored	☐	☐
10. I continue to actively learn new things	☐	☐

If you answer no to four or more of these questions, you may want to consult your doctor for steps to create a healthier lifestyle.

Develop Leisure and Lifestyle Interests

In addition to our dreams, we all have things we like to do just for fun. While some people are lucky enough to earn an income and fulfill a sense of purpose from an activity that started out as just an interest or a hobby, not all of us are that fortunate. That's OK. We still need to engage in activities that allow us to kick back, let our hair down and just have fun.

But with family and work obligations, many of us struggle to find time to fit pure fun into our lives. It seems there's always something more productive we could be doing. If that's you, it may be helpful to recognize the importance of leisure time in your life and then create a list of things you've always wanted to do. Call it your bucket list, your life list, or whatever you want. Include all those things - large or small - that you've always wanted to do. Then, as you complete different items on your list, you can cross them off with a feeling of productivity knowing that you've achieved a major life goal. If you'd like to create and track your life list online, you can also do that at Retirement2020.com.

My Life List

1. ______________________________

2. ______________________________

3. ______________________________

4. ______________________________

5. ______________________________

6. ______________________________

7. ______________________________

8. ______________________________

9. ______________________________

10. ______________________________

If you're having trouble, see the Interests and Activities Exercise included in Appendix 3 that will help you uncover meaningful activities to include on your life list.

The Role of Work

Understanding the role that a job will play in creating a vision or your ideal life depends on several factors. Obviously your financial situation and need to earn an income will be a huge factor, as will your dreams, personal purpose and satisfaction with your present job or career. As we consider this area, it's important to remember that our jobs - even if we don't particularly like them - play a huge role in our lives and often fulfill several of our key life arenas. Our personal identity, self-esteem, sense of purpose and social circles are often filled by where we work and what we do. Even our physical health and mental acuity are often impacted by our jobs.

Because so many of us are dissatisfied with our work, our jobs become one of the first areas we think about changing. But as you've probably begun to realize, there are a lot of steps you can take to improve other areas of your life that have nothing to do with your job. So while on the one hand it's critically important to have a job you enjoy - especially if your financial situation dictates you'll likely be working for another 15-20 years or so - it's also important not to make rash decisions and leave a job that provides good security and can become more fulfilling with a just a few small changes.

The first step in understanding how your job will fit into the vision of your ideal life is to evaluate your current employment. The following are just a few of the questions in the job section of the Life Planning Profile located at Retirement2020.com.

	Yes	Most of the time	Less than half of the time	No
1. I generally enjoy my job and what I do for a living.	☐	☐	☐	☐
2. My job energizes me so I can pursue other interests, it does not drain my energy.	☐	☐	☐	☐
3. The work I do is meaningful to me and provides a sense of purpose.	☐	☐	☐	☐
4. The things I'm asked to do at work are consistent with my values and beliefs.	☐	☐	☐	☐
5. I am able to apply my talents and interests at work.	☐	☐	☐	☐
6. I feel appreciated and valued for my contribution at work.	☐	☐	☐	☐
7. My job allows me sufficient time to pursue other interests. I have a good work-life balance.	☐	☐	☐	☐
8. I generally like the people I encounter through work (co-workers, clients, customers, etc).	☐	☐	☐	☐

If you are able to answer "Yes" or "Most of the time" to at least six of these questions, then chances are pretty good that only minor changes may be needed. Perhaps just a change in attitude or change in the daily tasks you perform will be enough to re-energize you and keep you moving forward. If on the other hand, you answer "Less than half the time" or "No" to five or more of the questions, you may need to look into a new company, a new industry or an entirely new career.

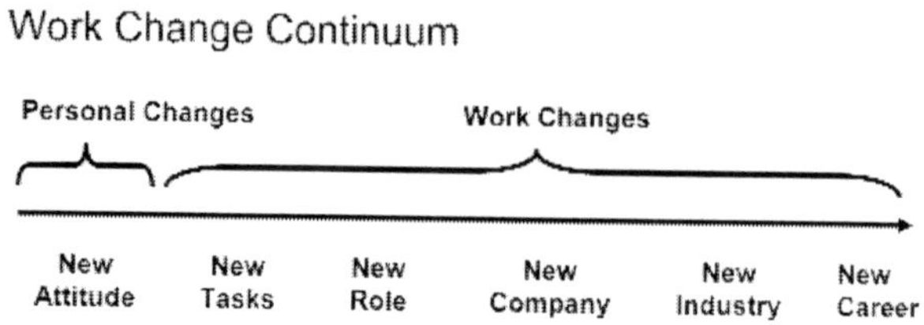

Figure 6.1
The Work Change Continuum

Figure 6.1 illustrates the work change continuum by showing the various steps that can be taken to improve job satisfaction. Oftentimes simply changing the tasks we perform at work can improve our work satisfaction. On one consulting project I was asked to analyze the efficiency of a financial advisor's practice. The team consisted of four individuals - the Senior Advisor, a Junior Advisor, a Sales Assistant and an Administrative Assistant. As I interviewed each member of the staff, I found the sales assistant to be highly disengaged from her job. She had been in her role for over 12 years and knew the job very well, but had become bored with it. The problem was she felt stuck. She didn't want to take on the risk of becoming a commissioned sales person as full-time advisor, but she was tired of simply processing paperwork. Because the practice was growing and the two advisors were feeling overwhelmed, I suggested that her role be expanded to include meeting with certain clients. As she took on these new tasks (while appropriately dispersing other tasks to other members of the team) she blossomed with these new responsibilities. Now she was able to meet with clients, develop deeper relationships and gained a renewed sense of purpose in her work. Her role and her position did not change, but by adding certain tasks to her current job, she was able to re-engage in her current work.

When small changes don't do the trick, we may have to look for opportunities to change our role within our current organization. In a similar situation several years ago I had the opportunity to promote a sales assistant into the role of a financial advisor. While this individual worked in the same office with the same people she had worked with for the past five years, her role now was completely different. Instead of executing plans that others had developed, she was now meeting with clients and developing plans of her own. Her new role included more responsibility and more at-risk compensation, but it also included more satisfaction and reward as she too was able to develop deeper relationships with her clients.

Another option is that sometimes we simply find ourselves with the wrong company. One young client of mine loved his work as a graphic designer for a small advertising agency, but the environment created by two warring partners was too volatile. Every week would bring a new conflict over strategic direction, art direction, client responsibilities or something similar. My client just wanted to do his job, but the tension made the situation simply unbearable. After 15 months he moved to a new firm and now loves his job.

It also happens that sometimes we even outgrow our companies. The fact is that as we change and develop new interests and skills, the people we work most closely with don't always recognize or value those changes. We often become pigeonholed by those people who assign us to a certain role within the organization and fail to see how much more we could contribute. Our desire to create more meaning and purpose is stifled by the organization's inability to see our expanding potential. When that becomes the issue, it's time to take your career ladder to a new company.

The next step on the change continuum is to take your existing specialty and apply it to a new industry. One of the best known examples of this is the story of John Sculley, an American businessman who in the 1970's used his marketing and managerial expertise to rise through the ranks to eventually become president of PepsiCo. In the early 1980's Steve Jobs, co-founder of Apple Computer, began to court Sculley away from Pepsi in hopes that Sculley would apply his marketing ingenuity on behalf of Apple to the personal computer market. Sculley finally agreed to take the reins at Apple after Jobs reportedly asked him, "Do you want to spend the rest of your life selling sugar-water or do you want a chance to change the world?" Clearly Sculley had chosen the right career path, but a change in industry offered him an opportunity to fulfill a more satisfying purpose.

The final step on our change continuum is to explore a new career. Now before you go here, it's important to explore all of your options within the previous, smaller change options that we've described. Starting over into an entirely new career is not for the faint of heart and requires a tremendous amount of effort, but if that is what your heart truly calls you to do, then the rewards will be well worth the effort.

One of the best resources available to those who are considering a career change is the Occupational Information Network (O*Net - http://online.onetcenter.org) developed under the sponsorship of the US Department of Labor/Employment and Training Administration (USDOL/ETA) through a grant to the North Carolina Employment Security Commission. With information on over 950 different occupations, the O*Net web site offers a number of career exploration tools designed to help you assess your interests and skills, identify occupations of interest, and provide information on both the requirements to enter a particular field and what to expect once you get there.

One of the most useful tools on the O*Net web site is an Ability Profiler assessment tool (http://www.onetcenter.org/AP.html). Many people who have spent most of their adult lives in one specific career or occupation tend to pigeon-hole themselves, thinking that their skills are only applicable to that one occupation or industry. The O*Net Ability Profiler measures nine job-relevant abilities and then cross references those abilities with their occupational database. By taking the assessment and comparing your results with the requirements of the field you hope to go into, you can begin to get an idea of where to begin your process for making a career change.

Other Resources

If going through these exercises doesn't give you the basis for defining your ideal life, more exploration may be necessary. There are several additional tools available that you may want to try.

Myers Briggs Type Indicator

Based on the work of psychiatrist Carl Jung, the Myer-Briggs Type Indicator (MBTI) was originally published in 1962 as a way to help people identify the type of work in which they would be most comfortable and effective. Over the years, the MBTI has become one of, if not the most widely used personality tests in the world.

The core of the MBTI is the identification of our individual preferences/tendencies within each of four opposite pairs, or dichotomies. Just as we are born with a preference for either right-handedness or left-handedness, so too, according to Jung and MBTI, are we born with preferences or tendencies within these four dichotomies. The four dichotomies include our preferences or tendencies toward introversion (I) or extraversion (E - as spelled in MBTI language), sensing (S) vs. intuition (N), thinking (T) vs. feeling (F) and judging (J) vs. perceiving (P). The preference of one or the other within each of the four dichotomies produces a four letter personality type (for example - ISTJ) that can be used to describe our natural tendencies.

Usually administered by a licensed or certified specialist, there are also several abbreviated versions of the MBTI available online. For more information, visit myersbriggs.org/.

Holland Codes

Formulated by psychologist John L. Holland, the Holland Codes also provide insight into what types of careers or vocations our personalities would be best suited. Unlike the MBTI, which produces 16 distinct personality types, the Holland Codes use six indicators ranked in terms of dominance within one's personality to produce 720 different personality patterns. The six personality indicators described by Holland include:

- ❖ **Realistic** - practical, physical, hands-on, tool-oriented
- ❖ **Investigative** - analytical, intellectual, scientific, explorative
- ❖ **Artistic** - creative, original, independent, chaotic
- ❖ **Social** - cooperative, supporting, helping, healing/nurturing
- ❖ **Enterprising** - competitive environments, leadership, persuading
- ❖ **Conventional** - detail-oriented, organizing, clerical

The individual's "code" is then created using the first letter of each indicator placed in order of its dominance (i.e. - RIASEC or AIESCR). Holland himself created two assessment tools called The Vocational Preference Inventory and the Self-Directed Job Search. His work has also been adopted by the U.S. Department of Labor for categorizing jobs relative to interests. More information can be found at the Occupational Information Network (O*Net) web site at onetcenter.org/.

Clifton StrengthsFinder

Based on the idea of accentuating strengths (as opposed to attempting to develop and therefore compensate for weaknesses) the StrengthsFinder program was initiated in 1998 in joint collaboration between Psychologists Donald Clifton and Tom Rath, and the Gallup Organization.

Updated in 2007, the StrengthsFinder 2.0 uses a series of questions to identify individual strengths among 34 classifications of talent. The top five themes are then used to provide guidance on the type of work or career for which you might be most well-suited. For more information visit strengthsfinder.com.

Bringing it all Together

By now you should be starting to get a good idea of what your ideal life looks like. You've examined your dreams, your purpose, your relationships and each of the other key life arenas. You've begun to identify your values and priorities, and to identify steps you can take to begin improving your life in each area.

At this point, the question many of you will be asking is, "How am I going to financially pull this off?" The answer is to practice Financial Maturity, which is topic of the rest of this book.

Chapter 7

Financial Freedom: A State of Mind

Now that you're beginning to get an idea of what your ideal life looks like, the question you're probably beginning to ask is how you're ever going to afford it. The reality is that our imaginations can usually come up with much more than our pocket books can support. But as you go through the Six Key Life Arenas in the previous chapter, it becomes easy to see that some of the most important aspects of our lives require very little money.

That's why creating your own personal financial freedom is more about examining your own priorities, attitudes and beliefs about money than it is about accumulating a certain amount of wealth. As I learned from Tom and Sue, the couple from Chapter 5 who retired very young with less accumulated assets than I would have expected, clearly defining your priorities, adopting healthy attitudes and beliefs, and then exercising the discipline to hold fast to those priorities is key to creating financial freedom. Just as Zig Ziglar talked about when discussing the priorities of have, do and be, having a lot of money doesn't create financial freedom. We need to *be* the kind of person who has a healthy relationship with money before we can *have* the financial freedom we want. What kind of person has a healthy relationship with money? The Financially Mature.

As we touched on earlier, Financial Maturity starts with understanding your attitudes and beliefs about money, so that's where we'll begin.

One-Sentence Lessons

Money plays an all-encompassing role in our lives. As mentioned, virtually every major decision we make involves some consideration of the monetary consequences. What we do, where we live and who we associate with are all impacted by our attitudes and beliefs about money. Where do those beliefs come from? Often, they come from childhood or cultural experiences that taint our perspective. Let me give you an example.

When I was 12 years old, a buddy called me on the phone one day and told me that an elderly neighbor woman had offered to pay him $20 to mow her lawn. He said that if I would help him, he would split the money with me. When we arrived, it looked as if her lawn hadn't been mowed all season. The grass was easily a foot high and there were broken tree branches and trash scattered all around. For the next four hours we pushed an old beat-up mower around her yard, raked and bagged at least a dozen bags of clippings and picked up all the branches and trash. When we finished, my friend and I walked to the front door, knocked and waited to collect our pay. When the woman answered the door, she didn't even bother to open the screen door, but tilted her head to one side to look around the corner and said, "You didn't do a good enough job. I'm not paying!" With that she slammed the door in our faces.

The lesson I learned that day was that people are not always fair when it comes to money. Sometimes that lesson has served me well when I've been confronted with situations that looked shady, and other times that lesson has harmed me when I've failed to trust someone who in fact deserved my trust.

Our world is filled with one-sentence lessons about money. I'm sure you've heard many of the following:

- Money is the root of all evil
- A penny saved is a penny earned
- Money doesn't grow on trees
- If you have everything you want, others won't have enough

- Talking about money is in poor taste
- Wealthy people are dishonest
- Money is a scorecard - more is better
- Save your money for a rainy day
- Money only comes to those who work hard
- Carpe diem! Live for today!
- Money is fair - it goes to those who earn it
- The system is built so the rich get richer

As you read this list, you may find yourself nodding in agreement with some of these statements, and shaking your head in disbelief about others. "How can someone believe that?" you may ask. The answer is in understanding yours and other's money personalities.

Of Eagles and Condors

Over the years I've watched hundreds of people struggle with various misplaced beliefs about money. Some believe that money truly does make the world go round while others truly believe it to be the root of all evil. For a long time I failed to recognize any pattern or consistency to these various beliefs until I read the book *The Soul of Money* by Lynne Twist, in which she related the story of an ancient Incan prophecy. The Prophecy of the Eagle and the Condor has been passed down among indigenous tribes of North and South America from generation to generation for hundreds of years. It goes something like this:

In the beginning, all the earth's people were as one - with one mind, one goal and one common interest. But long ago, the people divided into two groups and began to grow and develop in different ways. One group, the people of the Eagle, was highly scientific and intellectual. The people of the Eagle began to develop wondrous and miraculous technologies that advanced medicine, transportation, communication and construction. They utilized the earth's resources to create ever greater technologies that vastly improved their lives and brought abundant wealth to themselves and their leaders. With their dependence and emphasis on science, however, the people of the Eagle began to rely more and more on what they could see, hear or touch, and less and less on what they could inwardly sense or feel. While outwardly the people of the Eagle lived a wealthy and prosperous life, inwardly they became restless. They had lost touch with the great spirits and felt an emptiness in their souls that no amount of wealth could satisfy.

The other group, the people of the Condor, took an opposite path. They began to develop a deep connection with the natural world and developed highly intuitive skills. They began to see and understand the tremendous wonders of the natural world, and the great cycles of the earth. They began to feel, sense and understand their connection with the spirits, and see their role as one of many interconnected parts that fit together to create the wholeness of the universe. Inwardly, they were comfortable in their knowledge of their place in the greater scheme, but outwardly, theirs was a hard and difficult life. The people of the Condor failed to fully utilize the earth's resources to improve their physical condition, and as a result suffered much illness and toiled in difficult conditions just to survive.

One night a great shaman appeared in the dreams of the leaders of both peoples. To the leaders of the people of the Condor, the shaman congratulated them on their mastery of the laws of nature, but warned that their way of life was in danger. The people of the Eagle, he warned, would continue to consume the earth's resources until the people of the Condor were driven to extinction. To the leaders of the people of the Eagle, the shaman praised them on their advanced technology, but warned that without a sense of their place in the natural order, their empire would crumble in a downward spiral of greed, hatred, conflict and war.

To both groups of leaders, the shaman foretold of a time when the people of the Eagle and the people of the Condor would reunite in peaceful harmony, but not without first suffering tremendous conflict and pain. The people of the Eagle would push the people of the Condor to the brink of extinction, thereby assuring their own destruction as well. Only when each brought their gifts fully and without condition to the other, would peace begin to flourish. The people of the Eagle would bring the technologies that made their physical lives more comfortable, while the people of the Condor would bring the teachings of the earth and the insights to the spiritual world that gave them peace of mind and inner strength. With each contributing what it had learned to the other, a new age of peace and prosperity would emerge for all. For while each had developed a mastery of their own world, neither could survive without the other. Only when the Eagle and the Condor fly together in the open sky, said the shaman, can the world be in harmony.

So what has this got to do with financial freedom and creating your ideal life in the 21st century? Actually quite a lot. Let me explain.

After 20 years in the financial services industry I've come to believe that in matters of money, each of us is naturally inclined as either an Eagle or a Condor. We approach money as either a resource to be intellectually managed, mastered and controlled like the people of the Eagle, or as a force all its own to be trusted with natural rules, rhythms and cycles, as with the people of the Condor. Just as both peoples were able to accomplish great things on their own; in the end each approach was incomplete. They each needed the other's perspective to fully develop their culture to its highest potential. On a personal level, that's what each of us needs to do as well.

Just as the people of the Eagle put their belief in their intellectual skills to make their physical lives more comfortable, financial Eagles rely on their money skills to save and invest, believing that the accumulation of wealth will create the security and freedom they seek. But as we discussed in Chapter 4, no amount of wealth can create the emotions of freedom and security. Equally true, no amount of wealth can create the satisfaction and fulfillment that comes from a sense of contribution and purpose that define the vision of retirement today. For financial Eagles, when the belief is held too tightly, just the opposite happens. The overpowering accumulation addiction causes many Eagles to spiral into greed or fear. Not only are extreme Eagles obsessed with acquiring more, but they are also desperately afraid of losing what they already have.

For the financial Condor, the belief that the world of money is a force all its own that can be observed but not controlled provides them an excuse for their lack of money. Condors – usually subconsciously – believe the world of wealth is beyond both their reach and control. As such, any attempt to manage that world is futile. Condors will say there is no point in attempting to accumulate wealth as the natural order of the universe dictates they remain in their poor and downtrodden position. They often feel helpless in managing their resources and feel they either don't need or deserve anything beyond what's required to meet their basic needs. This belief often expresses itself in comments like, "I don't need money to be happy," or "Those who have money must have compromised their ethics to get it." Since they feel they cannot control the world of money, Condors tend to sit back and "let things take care of themselves."

If we were to go back and examine the one-sentence lessons discussed earlier, we begin to see how those various attitudes and beliefs are really reflections of financial Eagle or Condor personalities. "Money is the root of all evil" is clearly a financial Condor belief, just as "a penny saved is a penny earned" is an Eagle belief. Go back and look at each of the beliefs listed earlier and see if you can identify which are Eagle beliefs and which are Condor beliefs. (Appendix 4 provides the answers.)

Maslow and the Incans

If creating your ideal life means achieving self-actualization as Maslow suggested, it will take the skills of both the Eagle and the Condor within yourself to make those dreams real.

If we look once again at Maslow's hierarchy, we notice that the physiological needs of level one, are *tangible* needs, while the higher needs of levels three, four and five are *intangible* needs. The level two needs for security are both tangible in terms of protecting your physical self, and intangible in terms of creating a sense of financial security.

Figure 7.1
Maslow's Hierarchy

When we look at how we go about meeting these needs in our 21st-century world, we begin to see the roles – and limitations – that money has in our lives. Today we use money to meet our tangible, physiological needs for food, water, shelter, etc. As we discussed, most of us no longer hunt or farm for our own food. Remember that it wasn't until 1920 that more Americans lived in cities than on farms in the United States. Before then, the majority of the population lived and worked on farms as opposed to the factories. At that time, life on the farm was very different than it is even for today's farmers. In 1900, living on a farm meant growing enough food for your own family's survival, and hopefully selling what you had left over to put a few coins in your pocket. Meeting one's own basic needs consumed much of a person's time and energy throughout their lives. As a result, relatively few people were able to progress all the way up Maslow's hierarchy simply because their attention was constantly drawn toward meeting their most basic needs.

With the Industrial Revolution and the migration of the U.S. population from the farms to the cities, it became easier to meet those physiological needs. Instead of tending the fields for wheat and flour that we would bake into bread ourselves, we could now go to the store and purchase bread already made for us. As manufacturing, transportation and distribution processes became more efficient, it became easier and easier to meet those most basic needs. That is, of course, if you had the money to purchase the things you needed.

The net effect is that the tools required to meet our most basic needs changed from the plow and the hammer to money. I no longer need to know how to plant and raise a crop, or use a hammer to build a house, I just need to know how to acquire and use money to purchase the things I need. Now don't get me wrong, it is not as if money is a new invention or a new tool. Money has been around for ages. But it is fair to say that the widespread distribution of wealth created by global industrialization within just the last 100 or so years has allowed millions upon millions of people to dedicate themselves to tasks *other* than basic survival skills.

In fact, just like the people of the Eagle, it is the very fact that we have been able to more easily meet our most basic needs that has allowed our society to develop. Money has become an enabler. It provides each of us with freedom and opportunity. Not in a way that says if you accumulate enough of it you will never have to work again, but rather as a way to create value using our unique gifts and talents so we can trade that value for the things we need to survive.

For example, a genetic researcher could never trade his research to a farmer in return for food, nor could a software engineer trade her code for a place to live. Without money, what need would the farmer or landlord have for lab research or software code? Without money as a means to exchange those unique contributions, what place would there be in our society for those gifts? And yet, look at how much benefit the genetic researcher and software engineer have contributed to our society. By creating a means to exchange our personal value contribution in return for food, shelter, and the other things we need to survive, money provides us the freedom and opportunity to live our lives in pursuit of whatever vocation our heart calls us to.

For the financial Eagle, with their need to control, manage and master the world around them, learning to use money as a tool to meet their basic needs is often a straightforward task. They understand the mechanics of what they need, they know the rules about how to get there and they work to achieve the goal. It's as simple as that. Satisfying the higher-level needs is where Eagles often struggle. Like a mouse that's been trained to navigate a maze to get the cheese, Eagles continues to rely on the same money beliefs and practices that led them to satisfy their lower-level needs. When the cheese is moved, the mouse will continue to retrace the same steps over and over again in hopes that the next time they round that last corner, the cheese will be there. Likewise, the route (the tools – money) that allowed Eagles to meet their lower-level, tangible needs is not the same route necessary to meet the higher-level intangible needs.

Since the accumulation of money and wealth satisfied the previous, lower-level tangible needs, the financial Eagle continues to subconsciously believe that the accumulation of even more money and more wealth will satisfy the new higher-level intangible needs. Like the mouse, the Eagle becomes very confused and frustrated when the activities that once led to success no longer do so. Like the people of the Eagle, financial Eagles need to adopt the traits of the Condor and learn to trust in the world around them if they hope to reach Maslow's highest levels or create the ideal life of their dreams.

For the Condor, the struggle is often simply in getting sufficiently off of the first level. Many Condors have simply not learned how to use money as a tool to meet those most basic needs. The reasons are varied, but certainly include a set of misplaced beliefs about the role of money in our lives. For many years, our culture held a stigma that told us it was not polite to talk about money. Even parents felt uncomfortable teaching their children about money, perhaps because they themselves were not as educated on the subject as they would have liked. Regardless of the reason, entire generations of Condors have been raised without the knowledge of how to use the tools required to meet their most basic needs. Before the industrialization of society, parents taught their children how to hunt, how to farm and how to build a home. Children were taught how to use the tools they needed to survive. Today, a lack of financial education leaves many without the basic skills necessary to survive in today's world.

This lack of financial stability causes a great deal of frustration for many financial Condors. Remember, according to Maslow, only after a need has been met can the individual begin to move to the next level. However, at times when a lower-level need is temporarily no longer being met, the individual must descend the pyramid to address the deficiency before resuming their previous level. The desire to fulfill the previous higher level, however, does not go away. It is simply suspended for the time being until the lower-level need is satisfied.

For the Condor who begins moving up the pyramid, their satisfaction comes not from the accumulation of wealth but from the activities they pursue and the relationships they cherish. Unfortunately, financial Condors are often prevented from fully engaging in those activities and fully developing those relationships as their attention is constantly drawn back to managing their inadequate finances or dealing with economic setbacks simply in order to survive. This constant downward drag prevents them from consistently maintaining their highest state and fully creating the life they truly want. Financial freedom for a Condor is a very real income-versus-expense struggle that requires both financial education and the examination of the beliefs that may be subconsciously sabotaging their financial stability.

The Struggles of Birds

Carl was a client of mine who came to me a few months before he planned to retire from his 30+ years as an engineer at a large technology firm. Carl was a classic Eagle. Intellectual by nature, Carl studied every angle of every decision he ever made - paying particular attention to those decisions that involved money. The decision to retire was the ultimate money decision.

On the surface, everything looked good for Carl to retire and for he and his wife Peggy to live comfortably on their retirement savings. While Carl had always earned a better-than-average salary, they lived well within their means, had always saved and budgeted for anticipated expenses, and always put money into their retirement accounts. Both Carl and Peggy were very well disciplined in their spending and had run countless scenarios in deciding how much income they needed at retirement. They had invested their retirement savings prudently and now, with a lucrative early retirement offer on the table from his employer, easily had more than enough to retire comfortably. The only question was when to pull the trigger.

The year however, was 1999. As luck would have it, Carl's job was deemed critical to the "Y2K" transition of his firm, so he agreed to accept the enhanced early retirement offer, but would delay his retirement for one year until the fall of 2000. As you might recall, as the new millennium unfolded, so did the stock market, and with it a small but psychologically important portion of Carl's retirement savings.

Carl had set for himself a goal of two million dollars in retirement savings. Through his careful budgeting and analysis, that was the amount he deemed as his number, the amount that would be "enough" for him to retire safely and securely. Even without the early retirement offer, Carl had well exceeded this amount, but now with the market declining he was coming closer and closer to his required minimum. As both the market declined and his agreed-upon retirement date approached, Carl began to panic. He became obsessed with the daily swings of the stock market. He began to call not only me, but several other financial advisors on an almost daily basis seeking guidance and advice on what to do. The reality is that Carl had invested rather conservatively, so his accounts were not suffering nearly as badly as the market as a whole, but this was little solace. For a man who had spent years saving, planning and feeling in control of his future, this market volatility that was not within his control sent him reeling.

As I watched the stress and tension continue to grow within Carl, I realized just how classically Eagle his behavior was. All his life he had approached money from a purely intellectual perspective. He had learned about saving, investing and managing his expenses - all very positive skills necessary for success. But he failed to understand that the security he was seeking was an emotion, a state of mind that no amount of logic or money could create. He had put his faith in a system designed around numbers, and now that that system was failing him, he had nowhere to put his faith and trust.

Many of you might be thinking, "Two million dollars - that should be more than enough!" while others of you will be thinking,

"How can he possibly expect to retire on so little?" The fact is, the number is irrelevant. Very few Eagles ever believe they have enough. That's one of the basic clues that you might be an Eagle. If you have $500,000, you feel you need $700,000. If you have $5 million, you feel you need $7 million.

For as much as the world tries to convince us that the accumulation of great wealth is the key to happiness, security and the "good life," this is simply not true. Our highest needs - love, belonging, self-esteem, security and a sense of purpose - can never be met by any amount of zeros on an account statement. Yet many of us, and I must admit that for years I would have included myself among them, devote our lives to the belief that if we can just work a little harder, save a little more, or invest a little better, we'll finally someday become happy and secure. We spend our entire lives pursuing this goal only to wake up one day to realize the vision was a mirage. The path of endless accumulation that so many of us find ourselves on doesn't lead to the happiness and security we so desperately seek.

For Carl, even though he still had more than enough to retire on, that lack of faith and trust led him to a bitter battle with his employer to keep his job. In the end, he was forced to leave on the agreed-upon date but immediately went to work for another company after his retirement.

The Other Side of the Story...

Another client, Kathryn, was in her early-50s when she first came to see me. Kathryn had been married to a successful executive for 20 years, but had gotten divorced approximately two years before we met. Because her husband had earned a very good income, Kathryn chose not to pursue her own career during her marriage but instead had been actively involved in several charitable organizations. She was particularly involved in a local women's shelter and served on both its board of directors and as a member of the volunteer staff. After the divorce, Kathryn received a comfortable settlement and ongoing support that allowed her to continue, for the time being, her involvement with the various charities.

During her marriage, Kathryn's husband had handled all the family's finances, which was fine with her, as paying the bills and balancing a checkbook were not tasks she enjoyed or felt were particularly important. Even after the divorce, Kathryn continued to focus her time and energies on the various charities and spent as little time as possible managing her personal finances. As she would later tell me, "Dealing with that money felt dirty. It reminded me of failure. But working at the shelter made me feel good about myself." Still somewhat in a state of denial about her failed marriage, Kathryn used her work at the shelter to maintain her self-esteem and support the illusion that very little in her life had actually changed.

The reality of course, is that things had changed. She had kept the large house, but had no idea of the utilities, maintenance or taxes that were needed to maintain the house. Even though she was greatly valued for her work at the shelter, she refused to apply for a salaried position when one opened up. Kathryn certainly did not live extravagantly, but neither did she scale back her spending or examine her monthly cash flow. Slowly but surely, she began to see her settlement balances gradually decline as her support payments failed to keep pace with her normal living expenses.

Having worked so closely in the shelter, Kathryn was well aware of what happened to those women who had no financial resources. The sudden realization that if she didn't change her ways she could end up a client of the very shelter she supported is what motivated her to set up a meeting with me.

Kathryn, as you might guess, was a classic Condor. More intent on the greater good, Kathryn failed to learn and apply the basic skills necessary to secure her own financial future, and as a result, risked putting herself in a position where she might no longer be able to do the work that provided her a sense of purpose and fulfillment. As well-intentioned as most Condors are, their weakness lies in failing to fully utilize the resources - human and financial - available to them. By failing to fully utilize those resources, Condors limit their own ability to develop themselves to their fullest potential and achieve their highest, most heartfelt goals.

Just as the shaman foretold, the key to our personal peace, happiness and prosperity lies in developing the strengths of both the Eagle and the Condor within ourselves. While doing so is often a lifetime quest, those who do eventually develop both sets of skills achieve a level of financial security and financial freedom - what I call Financial Maturity - that allow them to effectively utilize money to achieve their highest goals and not be consumed by the stress and anxiety of financial worries. Fortunately, most of us have elements of both the Eagle and Condor already within us, but tend to lean more heavily to one side or the other. The goal is to create that 50/50 balance between the two as shown in figure 7.2 below.

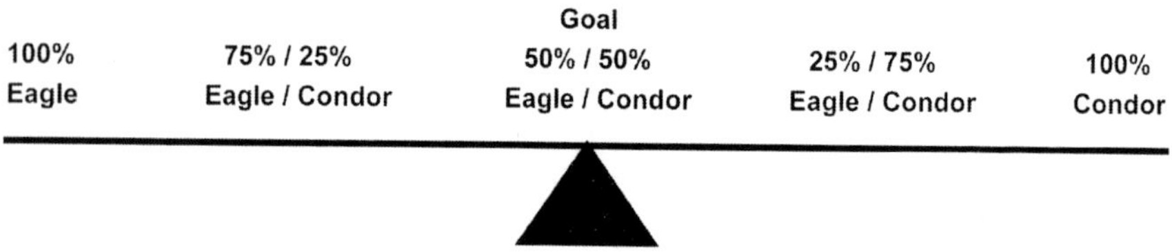

Figure 7.2
Eagle / Condor Personality Spectrum

Chapter 8

The Financial Pyramid

There are literally thousands of books on the market about how to manage your money, invest more wisely or get rich quick utilizing whatever tools and techniques the author has to offer. To be fair, some of these are quite good. But most simply prey off the fear and greed so deeply ingrained in most Eagles. They feed the accumulation addiction and perpetuate the belief that more is better. The promise that by following their "revolutionary new technique" you too can create a life of wealth and prosperity, as if accumulating more and more money is *the* key to happiness and success. As we've seen, it takes much more than money to be happy and content.

But that's not to say that money is not important. As one client said to me one day, "I've lived with money and I've lived without money. I can tell you, living with money is better." I don't disagree. The fact is that money is a necessity, and managing it is an essential modern-day survival skill.

For the financial Eagle, the challenge of overcoming the accumulation addiction and learning to trust in things beyond our control often requires a change in perspective, attitudes and beliefs. Often just being made aware of the issue is enough to begin that process. For financial Condors however, the challenge is in educating themselves about how money works so they can begin to build a solid financial foundation. That knowledge and education around matters of personal financial are the second element in creating Financial Maturity, and along with preparation and discipline will be the focus of the second half of this book.

This chapter covers the very basics of financial education. Some financial Eagles may find this information too basic and if so,

I invite you to skip ahead to Chapter 9. But for the financial Condors, I hope to provide the basics of financial education in such a way as to remove the mystery and provide you with the confidence to begin moving yourself forward.

The Financial Planning Pyramid

Before we dive too deeply into the details of personal finance, it's helpful to take a step back and look at the big picture from a 30,000 foot level. Like Maslow, the financial planning community also uses a pyramid to illustrate the basic building blocks necessary to create financial security.

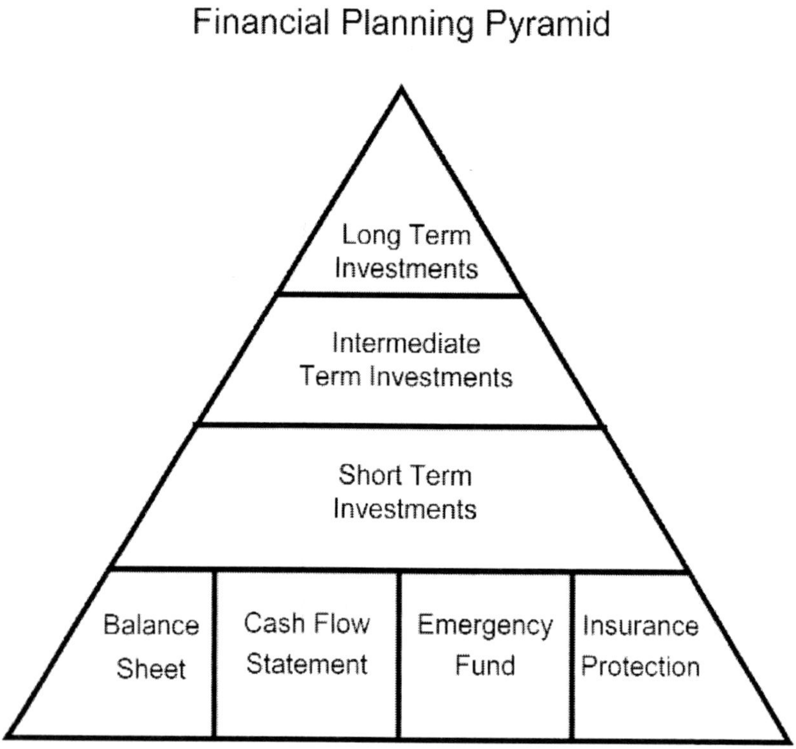

Figure 8.1
The Financial Planning Pyramid

You may have seen more complicated financial planning pyramids, but the reality is that this is all it boils down to. More advanced concepts such as estate planning and tax planning are beyond the scope of this book and often include strategies utilizing the tools in this pyramid. As mentioned, this chapter is intended to provide a basic financial education.

The foundation of your financial security is made up of four blocks - your personal financial statements, which include a balance sheet and cash flow statement, an emergency fund, and your insurance protection. Too often people become anxious and start investing before they take care of these basics. In classic Condor fashion, they hope to cash in quickly through investments that they don't fully understand without having established a solid foundation first. Seldom do these "sure-thing" investments work out and the Condor is stuck with yet another financial setback. While these first four items that make up your financial foundation aren't sexy, they are necessary to make sure that everything you begin to build on top of them is supported and not in danger of collapse.

To illustrate, let's look at a couple named Mark and Julie. They were in their mid-30s and had been living the good life. They both had great jobs making good money and they liked to travel and have nice things. They lived in an upscale neighborhood, drove expensive cars and dressed very well. Because they both had well-paying jobs, they never had to worry too much about tracking their spending. Their combined paychecks always seemed to keep enough in the checking account to allow them to do whatever they wanted, and their credit cards were usually paid in full each month.

Unfortunately, Mark and Julie had racked up quite a bit of debt in school loans when they were both in college, so they delayed contributing to their company's 401(k)s until they got their student loans paid off. When the student loans were finally paid off, they decided to treat themselves to an expensive vacation, delaying their enrollment into their 401(k)s even further. Finally one day, Mark decided he wanted to get serious about saving for retirement. He had spoken with several friends who were about his same age and same stage in their careers and they all had sizeable 401(k) balances. Mark began to feel as if he were "behind" in his savings and decided that both he and Julie should start saving immediately.

At Mark's urging, both he and Julie enrolled in their company's 401(k) plans to the maximum 15% of pay contribution the plans would allow. Eighteen months later, they came in to see me because they had begun fighting about money. It seems they had run up considerable credit card and consumer debt that they could no longer afford to pay off each month, as their paycheck amounts deposited into their checking accounts were reduced by their 401(k) contributions.

Mark and Julie had made the classic mistake of jumping ahead of themselves on the financial planning pyramid. They had begun to contribute to long-term investments, their 401(k) plans, without ever analyzing or understanding what impact that would have on their cash flow. They didn't adjust their spending patterns to account for the reduced income. And while they were accumulating one asset - their 401(k) plans - they were offsetting that asset with ever-increasing liability - the growing credit card debt. The net effect was that they were making no progress at all. Their net worth, the value of all their assets minus all their liabilities, hadn't increased at all even though they were now on a structured saving plan. Even though they now considered themselves "experienced" investors, they still needed to go back to the fundamentals to begin building true financial security.

We'll look at all the blocks in the pyramid in more detail a bit later, but let's start with just a quick overview.

The first two of the four basic building blocks upon which all of us begin to build our financial freedom is in getting a handle on our personal financial statements, which include a **Personal Cash Flow Statement (PCFS)** and a **Personal Balance Sheet (PBS)**. These two personal financial statements are the cornerstones upon which you will build your financial house.

The personal balance sheet is nothing more than a listing of all your assets (the things you own) and your liabilities (the loans on which you owe.) The total of all your assets minus the total of all your debts gives you your *net worth*. While many people tend to judge their financial progress based on their income - i.e. - if they received a 5% raise this year then they figure they must be doing well - you should judge your financial progress based on the increase in your net worth. It's not how much you make that's important, but how much you *keep*. For most financial Eagles, the personal balance sheet is the scorecard they keep.

The personal cash flow statement is also a listing of two items. In this case it's a listing of all your amounts and sources of income on one side, and all of your outgoing expenditures on the other. Whereas a personal balance sheet is a snapshot of your various account balances at any single given moment in time, a cash flow statement tracks your income and expenses *over* a period of time - typically one month. Obviously the hope is that your income over that time will be greater than or at least equal to all of your expenses for the same period. For Eagles and Condors alike, maintaining the discipline to control your spending is key to financial success. The personal cash flow statement will help you to track your monthly spending.

The third block that creates the foundation of your financial pyramid is an **Emergency Fund**. The emergency fund is a pool of money you keep in reserve so that when unexpected expenses come up, as they always seem to do, you have a place from which to draw extra money so as not to upset your cash flow or go further into debt. In that respect, the emergency fund serves as your financial safety net.

The fourth and final block that creates the foundation of your pyramid is to ensure you have adequate **Insurance Protection** on your most valuable assets. These include your life, health, disability, home, auto and a number of others we'll talk about later. While at times it feels we can be over-insured to death, the fact is that insurance is a necessary evil. Without it you're taking big risks that should anything happen, you could be wiped out and your best laid plans completely destroyed. Many people take that risk thinking "It'll never happen to me" but those are the people who often become statistics.

Once we have our foundation covered, we can begin to move up the pyramid into the world of investments. The first level consists of **Short-Term Investments** that include things like checking and savings accounts, money market accounts, certificates of deposit (CDs), and Treasury bills (T-bills). These types of investments typically carry very little risk to your principal, but also return very little to you in the form of interest. These types of investments are categorized as short term because they will typically be used for money that you know you will use within a short period of time.

Intermediate-Term Investments typically consist of things like bonds and bond mutual funds, balanced mutual funds and growth-and-income type funds, while **Long-Term Investments** include things like stocks, stock mutual funds and annuities. For our purposes here, commodities and options will be considered speculative investments beyond the scope of our discussion.

Understanding Your Personal Balance Sheet

Several years ago my then 8-year-old son Christopher and I were on a bike ride along one of the bike trails in town. We were riding a section that he had not been on before, and he was very curious to explore where this trail was heading. After a short distance, we came upon a large trail map sign. He intently studied the map and after a few moments said, "We must be here," while pointing to a specific spot on the map. I looked at the map and the spot where he was pointing and asked, "Are you sure?" He studied the map another moment and then sheepishly said, "Oh, I guess we're here," pointing to a big X, "You are here," marker on the map just a short distance away from his original guess.

Within another mile or two, we came upon another sign. Again, Christopher insisted we stop so he could study the map and track our progress. Now that he recognized the "You are here," markers, it was easy for him to determine just how far we had come, and how much further we had to go to the end of the trail. As we continued down the trail, he insisted we stop at every one of those map signs to track our progress along the way.

A personal balance sheet (PBS) is a lot like those "You are here," markers on the map. It is simply a snapshot telling you where you are at any given point in time. By itself, a PBS will not tell you if you are heading in the right direction, or how close you are to achieving your goals, it is simply a statement of where you are at that particular moment. Only when you compare a past PBS to a current PBS, can you begin to determine the direction you are heading.

A personal balance sheet is nothing more than a listing of all assets and debts that a person or family owns (as is the case with an asset) or owes (as is the case with a debt.) All assets are listed on the left hand side of the page, (or in some formats, the upper part of the page) and all the debts are listed on the right hand side (or lower portion) of the page, as shown Figure 8.2.

Balance Sheet			
Assets		**Debts**	
Asset 1	$1,000	Debt 1	$ 500
Asset 2	$1,500	Debt 2	$1,500
Asset 3	$2,500		
Total Assets	$5,000	Total Debts	$2,000
Net Worth: Total Assets minus Total Debts = $3,000			

Figure 8.2
Personal Balance Sheet

When creating your PBS, you simply list the asset or debt and its corresponding value on that date. Usually it's best to take the values of all of your asset and debt accounts as of the same date, as this will give you a more accurate snapshot of where you are at any given time.

For example, it would not make sense to list an asset value from a recent statement, and a debt value from a statement that is six months old. By listing values as of the same or very similar dates, you create a more accurate statement. When you have listed all of your assets and debts, you will want to total each column to come up with a total dollar figure for each. By subtracting the total of all debts from the total of all assets, you get a number that is known as your net worth. By comparing your net worth figure from one PBS statement to another over time, you can get a feel for how you are progressing. An increasing net worth is a sign of financial progress, whereas a decreasing net worth may be cause for concern and investigation.

To begin to use this information however, we need to know more than just what and how much we have. We also need to know what type of assets and debts we have as not all assets and not all debts are created equally. Different types of assets have different characteristics and are used for different purposes, just as different types of debts also have various characteristics and purposes. Let's start by examining the different types of assets.

If we add a level of detail to the balance sheet, as we've done in Figure 8.3, you'll see that assets can be classified into three broad categories.

Balance Sheet	
Assets	**Debts**
Cash Flow Assets	
Investment Assets	
Other Assets	

Figure 8.3

Cash Flow Assets are things like checking accounts, savings accounts and money market accounts. These accounts are typically funded with short-term investments and are used to make your day-to-day purchases and pay your everyday bills. The goal of this money is to be both liquid and safe. Liquid (meaning readily available) so you can get to it at a moment's notice, and safe so that there is no fluctuation to your principal and it is there when you need it. We figuratively "pay" for these two features (safety and liquidity) in the form of a lower interest rate. That's OK. This money is typically short-term money so we are not as concerned about the rate of return we receive. Its primary purpose is to be there and available when we need it.

The second category is investment assets. These are the assets that you will eventually draw your retirement income from and build your future financial security around. These are things like your brokerage and investment accounts, 401(k)s, IRAs and rental real estate.

It's important at this point to understand the difference between the actual investments such as stocks, bonds and mutual funds that are inside the accounts and which we'll talk about in Chapter 9, and the accounts those investments are held in. When you invest in a stock, bond or mutual fund, you must first open an account at a brokerage firm, mutual fund company, insurance company or similar institution. The account is the place you actually hold the investment, not the investment itself. The account acts like a cup that you can then put any variety of investments into. Your account can hold different types of investments such as stocks, bonds or mutual funds. It's important to understand this, because different fees, penalties and taxes can be applied to either the account or the investment, and sometimes both. Too often people make the simple mistake of closing an account because they don't like the performance of an investment that is inside that account. In doing so, they often incur withdrawal penalties, taxes or tax penalties. It's like tossing out a very expensive china cup because you don't like the tea that was served. Just dump the investment and fill the account with a new investment more to your liking. The bottom line is to make sure you understand the fees and tax implications between the account and the investment before you make a move. Again, we'll talk about the various investments in Chapter 9 but for now we are simply concerned with understanding how the account itself works.

The account also does two other things of vital importance: It signifies both the ownership and tax treatment of the assets held in the account. The account registration lists the names of the account owner(s) and determines what happens to the account (i.e. - who gets it) when the account owners pass away. The account registration will also determine what type of tax treatment the account will receive regardless of what type of investment vehicle (stock, bond or mutual fund, etc) is inside the account.

To understand the tax treatment aspect further, our investment asset category can then be broken down further into qualified versus non-qualified accounts as shown in Figure 8.4.

Balance Sheet	
Assets	**Debts**
Cash Flow Assets Checking, Savings Money Markets, CD's Investment Assets Non-Qualified Qualified Other Assets	

Figure 8.4

Qualified accounts are those that receive (i.e. - *qualify for*) special tax treatment under IRS rules. These are typically intangible investment accounts such as 401(k)s or 403(b)s. While not technically considered qualified accounts, IRAs carry virtually identical basic characteristics, so we will include IRAs in this discussion as well. To understand what some of these special tax treatments are, it's helpful to define a few terms.

A **tax-deductible** account is one that allows you to deduct amounts contributed from your ordinary taxable income. Let's say you earn $50,000 per year from your employer but choose to contribute 10% ($5,000) of that to a tax-deductible 401(k). When preparing your income taxes you are allowed to deduct the $5,000 401(k) contribution from your taxable income and would be required to claim only the $45,000 as earned income, thereby reducing your current-year income taxes. If you had put the same $5,000 into a non-deductible account, you would be required to claim the full $50,000 as earned income.

Now let's assume you have the $5,000 in an account. Hopefully that account will earn some type of interest or dividend, which is also normally taxed. If the account is **tax-deferred** however, then the taxes due on the earnings generated by the account are deferred until some point in the future. Taking our previous example one step further, if your $5,000 were invested into a savings account earning 2%, you would receive $100 in interest throughout the year. Under normal circumstances in a non-tax-deferred account you would be required to claim that $100 as additional income on your yearly income tax return and pay ordinary income taxes on that $100. In a tax-deferred account, you could defer claiming that $100 of interest until some point in the future when you actually withdrew that money from the account.

Today, most 401(k)s offer both tax-deductibility and tax-deferral and as such are considered qualified accounts. Traditional IRAs are definitely tax-deferred and may be tax-deductible depending on whether you pass two tests. First, are you or your spouse (if applicable) eligible to contribute to an employer's qualified plan? If the answer is no, then you can deduct the amount you put into an IRA, up to specified IRS limits. If the answer to the first question is yes, you are eligible to contribute to an employer's qualified plan, then your eligibility to deduct contributions to a traditional IRA will be determined by your earned income and tax filing status. I won't go into the specific limits here, but more information can be found at http://www.irs.gov/publications/p590/ch01.html#en_US_publink10006139. A Roth IRA is always tax-deferred (assuming you meet certain age and length of time holding requirements) but is never tax-deductible.

As you can see, there are definitely significant tax advantages to most qualified plans. To receive this special tax treatment, however, there is a trade-off. Under current rules, the IRS requires that you leave your money inside these qualified accounts until you are 59 ½ years old. While there are some exceptions, generally any money withdrawn from a qualified account prior to age 59 ½ is subject to ordinary income taxes and a 10% penalty tax. Because combined federal and state ordinary tax rates often reach 30% or more, the addition of a 10% penalty often means losing 40% or more of your early withdrawal to taxes. For this reason, most financial advisors will recommend leaving your qualified money in these accounts until you reach age 59 ½ or are otherwise eligible to withdraw them without penalty.

Non-qualified accounts are simply those that do not qualify for any special tax treatment. The disadvantage of course is that you don't receive the benefits of tax-deferral or tax-deductibility. The advantage is that these accounts are not restricted by tax considerations and therefore are available for you to use at any time, for any reason you choose.

Because the tax treatment of qualified and non-qualified accounts is so different, it's important to differentiate between the two on your PBS. While putting money into qualified accounts will help to reduce your current tax burden due to the preferential tax treatment, your non-qualified accounts give you more flexibility today to use the money as you choose. Understanding the qualified status of your accounts and the amounts you have in each will help you to formulate and evaluate your options going forward.

The investment asset category also includes rental real estate and other types of tangible assets. For real estate to be considered an investment asset however, it must pass two tests:

1. It must have the *ability* to produce income.
2. It must have the *potential* to appreciate in value.

If it does not pass both these two tests, then it should not be considered an investment asset. Instead, it will likely fall into the third category - other assets.

Other assets are things like your home, other non-income producing real estate, cars, boats and other personal property. We tend to refer to these as "bad" assets because they don't pass *both* of the tests that investment assets do - produce income and have the potential to appreciate in value. Furthermore, these bad assets often have the nasty habit of *costing* you money in the form of interest paid on loans to acquire the asset, property taxes, licensing fees, maintenance, and so on.

Let's take home ownership for example. There is no doubt that millions of Americans have made millions of dollars worth of profit buying and selling their homes, so there is no question that your home is an asset. But as an asset, it has the potential to do just one of the things that investment assets do - appreciate in value. (Hopefully. There are also hundreds of thousands of homes in foreclosure because they didn't appreciate, but depreciated in value over the last few years, but that's another topic.) Since price appreciation is not guaranteed, the ability to produce income is required to be considered an investment asset. Most of us don't rent out the basements or any other portion of our homes to produce income from them, and therefore we shouldn't classify them as investment assets. If in fact you do rent out your home part of the year and generate an income from it, then you can reasonably classify your home as an investment asset.

This raises an important point: Let's also be clear that just because an asset is not considered a "bad" asset, that does not necessarily make it a "good" investment. A good investment is one that provides a reasonable rate of total return over time. Many investments that have the ability to produce income and the potential to appreciate in value often fail to do either. Those are clearly not good investments. Many homes on the other hand, based on price appreciation alone, are good investments. But if it doesn't pass the first test - to produce income - we won't call it an investment asset.

With all that said, it should come as no surprise then that things like cars, boats, and most other personal property are considered "bad" assets. They generate no income, usually depreciate in value, and cost you even more money to license or maintain. Instead of having the ability to bring cash flow *to* you, they'll typically cause cash to flow *away* from you. That's a bad asset.

When listing your other assets on your PBS, be sure to list it at its full current market value (i.e. what you could sell it for right now). Many people will mentally adjust that number to subtract a loan against the property, or tie its value to the property's purchase price. Unfortunately what you paid for it doesn't matter, and we'll deal with any loans against the property on the debt side of the PBS. For now, put down what you think you could sell it for at the time you create the PBS.

To add just a bit more detail then, the asset side of our personal balance sheet now looks like Figure 8.5.

Balance Sheet	
Assets	**Debts**
Cash Flow Assets Checking, Savings Money Markets, CD's Investment Assets Non-Qualified Qualified 401k, IRA, etc Other Assets Homes, Land Personal Property	

Figure 8.5

Let's now turn our attention to the debt side of the PBS. Like our assets, our debts can be divided into three categories: short-term debt, intermediate-term debt, and long-term debt. As the names imply, the distinction lies in the length of time it will take to pay off each type. When listing each debt, include the remaining balance owed as of the date of the PBS as the amount you list for each debt. For planning purposes you'll also want to note the amount of the monthly payment, the interest rate and the anticipated payoff date.

Short-term debts are usually things such as credit cards or personal loans that will be paid off within six months. Larger credit card balances or personal loans that will take longer to pay off are considered intermediate-term debt.

Intermediate-term debts typically include auto loans or leases, and many student loans that will be paid off within five years. Long-term debts include mortgages, real estate loans and any other loans or debts that will take longer than five years to completely repay. Figure 8.6 shows the debt side of a personal balance sheet.

Balance Sheet	
Assets	**Debts**
Cash Flow Assets Checking, Savings Money Markets, CD's	Short Term Debt Credit Cards
Investment Assets Non-Qualified Qualified 401k, IRA, etc	Intermediate Term Debt Auto Loans Student Loans
Other Assets Homes, Land Personal Property	Long Term Debt Mortgages Home Equity Loans

Figure 8.6

It's helpful to divide our debts into these timeframe-based categories so we can create a strategy to plan our cash flow around when each debt will be paid off, and when the corresponding monthly payment will be freed for other purposes. We'll discuss this more in the next section on the personal cash flow statement.

As mentioned earlier, when you add up the total of all your debts, and subtract that figure from the total of all your assets, the resulting number is your net worth. While many people tend to judge their financial progress from year to year based on the amount of income they earn, the real measure comes in watching your Net Worth. Your Net Worth grows by both accumulating assets (hopefully investment assets) and by paying down debts. Many people with large incomes have equally large expenses that do not allow them to save and grow their assets. Often these same people will leverage their assets with debts that obligate large portions of their income, further limiting their ability to save and invest. Others, who have very modest incomes, are able to control their expenses and carry very little debt, which allows them to save and grow their assets, which continue to grow their net worth.

Since a PBS is a snapshot of assets and debts at any given moment in time it does not show any trend by itself. But by comparing your PBS and bottom line net worth figure over a series of PBS's created over time, you can begin to judge your overall financial progress as you watch your net worth grow.

An excel spreadsheet of a personal balance sheet can be downloaded for free at Retirement2020.com/article.php?id=87

Understanding Your Personal Cash Flow Statement

As the second of the two personal financial statements a Personal Cash Flow Statement (PCFS) is vital to your financial security. A PCFS is nothing more than an accounting of all your cash inflows (income) and outflows (expenses) over a given period of time. Usually a PCFS is done on a monthly basis, but others are done quarterly, annually or semi-annually. The key is to make sure you do them often enough to maintain a strong understanding of your cash flow.

In terms of format, all sources and amounts of income for the timeframe being examined are listed on the left side of the page, (or in some formats, the upper part of the page) and all the expenses are listed on the right side (or lower portion) of the page, as shown in Figure 8.7.

Cash Flow Statement	
Income	**Expense**
Total Income minus Total Expenses = Net Cash Flow	

Figure 8.7
The Personal Cash Flow Statement

Subtracting your total expenses from your total income for the period will provide you with a net cash flow number. Obviously, a positive net cash flow (meaning income is more than expenses) is required to accumulate assets, pay off debts and build your net worth. Compared to the expense side of the PCFS, the income side is relatively simple, so let's start there.

All sources of income can be divided into three broad categories, earned income, investment income and other income as shown in Figure 8.8.

Cash Flow Statement	
Income	**Expense**
Earned	
Salary	
Investment	
Portfolio Income	
Rental Income	
Other	
Pension	
SS	

Figure 8.8

Earned income is compensation earned from participation in a trade or business, including wages, salary, tips, bonuses, self-employed income and other compensation. It's important to distinguish earned income from other types of income because earned income is subject not only to federal and state income taxes, but also to Social Security and Medicare taxes. Collectively known as FICA, these two taxes combine to take a 7.65% chunk out of all earned income up to certain amounts. The Social Security portion of FICA taxes is currently set at 6.2% of all earned income up to specified annual limits. The amount of earned income subject to the Social Security tax is set by the Social Security wage base of $106,800 for 2010. Medicare taxes are currently set at 1.45% on all earned income.

Understanding these taxes becomes even more relevant when we recall the Social Security discussion of Chapter 3. These are the taxes that fund our current Social Security retirement benefits. Based on the number of workers paying in and the current rate of 6.2%, the Congressional Budget Office now predicts that more money will be paid out in benefits beginning in 2010 than will be taken in from these payroll taxes. According to the 2009 Social Security Trustees report, *"an immediate and permanent increase of 2.01 percentage points"* would be required to maintain solvency for the next 75 years. Disregarding increases in Medicare for the moment, that would mean nearly 10% of earned income would go to FICA taxes. For employers and the self-employed who are required to match the employee's FICA tax contribution, the effect is doubled. Self-employed individuals in the future may reasonably expect nearly 20% of their earned income to go toward Social Security and Medicare taxes.

The issue becomes something of a cultural catch-22. Remember that these calculations also include an assumption about the number of people working and therefore contributing and paying into the system. As more workers delay their retirement and continue to work, more money will be contributed to the system, thereby potentially reducing the amount of increase necessary to stabilize the system. For the individual who spent their life in a job they dislike hoping to retire at 65 or sooner however, the prospect of working another 10 years to "sustain the system" seems a bitter pill to swallow.

Investment income, for purposes of our PCFS, includes any income withdrawn from the investment assets of our personal balance sheet. For our investment portfolios of stocks, bonds, mutual funds or other intangible financial assets, this income can come in the form of dividends, interest or even systematic withdrawals of principal. Income from rental real estate properties is also considered investment income.

Unlike earned income, investment income is considered unearned and therefore is not subject to FICA taxes. It may however, be subject to other taxes. If, as discussed earlier, the account is considered qualified, then any withdrawals will be subject to ordinary income tax. If you are also less than age 59 ½ and do not qualify for any of the various exceptions, those withdrawals will also be subject to a 10% penalty tax. If the account is non-qualified, then any earnings will be subject to ordinary income tax whether you use it as income or reinvest it back into the account.

As you can see, the tax treatment of your investment income can be extremely complicated. I will not even attempt to discuss capital gain taxes, alternative minimum taxes or the special tax treatment given to municipal bonds. Suffice it to say however that distinguishing your income between qualified and non-qualified sources will help you to manage your tax burden and allow you to more efficiently utilize your resources to achieve the life you want to lead.

The last category of income - other income - includes things such as any pensions you may receive and/or your Social Security benefits. These too have specific tax rules, but are usually based on the total amount of income you receive. As such there are fewer planning opportunities around these types of income. That said however, educating yourself around the tax implications and alternatives of all your sources of income is a critical step to ensuring you receive the most lifestyle benefit from your financial resources. This is an area where professional assistance is highly recommended.

The expense side of the PCFS can also be broken down into two broad categories, fixed expenses and variable expenses. Each of these is then divided even further as indicated in Figure 8.9.

Cash Flow Statement	
Income	**Expense**
Earned Salary Investment Portfolio Income Rental Income Other Pension SS	Fixed Expenses Savings Periodic Expenses Debt Service Recurring Variable Expenses Necessities Discretionary

Figure 8.9

Fixed expenses are those expenses that are a permanent, fixed part of your budget. The exact amount of the fixed expense may fluctuate, such as the exact amount of your phone or heating bill each month, but regardless of the amount, the expense will be there. As such, fixed expenses can be broken down into the following four subcategories.

Savings Expenses. While most people don't think of savings as an expense, the Financially Mature do. They know that the only way to accumulate wealth (other than have it given to you) is to save on a regular basis. As such, the first payment that should be made every month is to you. Set up separate accounts for each financial goal that you have - retirement, college education, vacation, new house, new car, etc. - and contribute to those accounts every month. Remember also to save in both qualified and non-qualified accounts to create flexibility and provide options for any future job or career changes you may consider.

One of the most critical savings expenses that you need to account for on a monthly basis is your emergency fund. Things happen in our lives that we don't expect, and they're often very expensive. Regularly contributing to and maintaining an emergency fund will help to avoid pulling out the credit card and going into further debt when unexpected expenses do occur.

Periodic Expenses. These are normal expenses that don't occur on a regular monthly basis. Many people choose to pay their insurance premiums, property taxes, homeowner's association dues and other expenses on an annual, semi-annual or quarterly basis. Even though these bills are not due each month, we need to accrue for these expenses by saving toward them each month. Credit unions and banks have long advocated this practice by offering Christmas club or vacation club accounts that allow you to save money toward a specific purpose throughout the year.

Debt Service. Debt service is simply the total amount of monthly payments required to pay back all the money you've borrowed. These include your mortgage, car payments, credit cards and all the other loans listed on the debt side of your personal balance sheet. For many people, monthly debt service consumes the majority of their monthly income. Unfortunately these are the same people who often say they feel trapped by their financial obligations. By paying off and limiting the amount of debt you carry you are able to free up more of your monthly cash flow, which allows you to pursue the things you truly want to do. We'll provide some strategies for paying off debt in a moment.

Recurring Expenses. The final type of fixed expense is your recurring expenses. Recurring expenses are those monthly bills such as utilities and insurance that pay for services as you use them. The amount of each recurring expense may vary from month-to-month, but unless you stop using the service (i.e. disconnect the phone) the bill will keep coming. Income taxes also fall into this category as you continue to incur some kind of income tax liability as long as you are earning an income.

The second broad category of expenses is your variable expenses, which can be broken down into necessity expenses and discretionary expenses. A distinguishing characteristic of variable expenses is that they often occur more than once per month.

Variable necessity expenses are things like food, basic clothing, transportation and medical expenses. The amounts may vary significantly from month-to-month, but unlike the phone or cable TV, we can't really choose not to eat. Often we'll make several trips to the grocery store, or fill the car up with gas every week. Monitoring our variable necessity expenses requires that we track our spending in these items throughout the month.

Variable discretionary expenses are where both the most problems and most opportunities lie. Variable discretionary expenses are things like dining out, entertainment and recreation. The problem with discretionary expenses is that these tend to be the source of "leaks" in our cash flow. The daily latte or impulse purchase often adds up to significant amounts over the course of a month. These leaks may or may not be adding significant satisfaction to our overall lifestyle. The opportunity lies in both curbing our discretionary spending on items that don't add to our overall lifestyle satisfaction, and consciously directing that spending toward things that will add to significantly increasing our satisfaction.

Because so much of our lifestyle satisfaction is derived from our discretionary spending, we should strive to increase the percentage of our income that we're able to comfortably allocate to it. Not, of course, by spending money we don't have, but by decreasing the amounts obligated elsewhere. Regardless of the amount of your total income, if 95% of it is obligated to debt service, recurring expenses and variable necessity expenses, there is little left over to support the things that add to your quality of life. You end up feeling trapped by your obligations. If, on the other hand, you've limited your total expenses to 50 or 60% of your total income or less, you now have excess disposable income that you can use to pursue those things that are truly meaningful to you. If you're looking to make a major life transition to a new career or retirement, reducing your total monthly expenses provides more options as to when you might be able to make that move.

When creating your PCFS, there are a couple of things to keep in mind:

1. Make sure you include ALL your expenses. Periodic expenses in particular have a tendency of being overlooked.
2. Don't count on income that isn't assured. Bonuses, commissions or other windfalls of income may not be consistent. If your cash flow would turn negative if those things were not present, it's likely you may be living a bit above your means.

You can download a Microsoft® Excel™ version of a Personal Cash Flow Worksheet at Retirement2020.com/article.php?id=88.

Creating an Emergency Fund

As the third block forming the base of the financial planning pyramid, an emergency fund is vital to ensuring that you can handle unexpected expenses as they arise. As one client - a financial Eagle, naturally - once told me, he budgeted his expenses so precisely that to him there was no such thing as an unexpected expense. That is, until his adult daughter moved back home with him. Like I said, life has a way of throwing us curveballs. An emergency fund gives you the ability to deal with them. Here are some tips on creating your emergency fund.

1. An Emergency Fund is a backup pool of money that usually consists of anywhere from three- to six-months worth of living expenses. As such, you need to know what your monthly living expenses are. By tracking your expenses with a monthly cash flow statement, you gain both the knowledge of what it takes to maintain your standard of living should your income be interrupted, and where you can cut back if you need to. This knowledge of what it takes and the preparation of having an emergency fund go a long way toward creating that peace of mind and confidence that comes with financial freedom.

2. Another factor in determining how much to have in your emergency fund is whether you are a one-income or two-income household, and a realistic expectation of how long it would take to secure another job if necessary. While loss of a job is not the only reason you may tap your emergency fund, it is one of the most common. If you are a one-income household or have a highly specialized job and live in an area with few opportunities to do what you do, you'll want to lean more toward a six-month (or longer if truly specialized) emergency fund. If you are a two-income household and have highly transferable skills and jobs are abundant, you may get by with only three months. The goal of course, is to have money readily available should your regular income stream be interrupted. You do not want to be forced to tap into qualified retirement accounts or other accounts you've established for specific goals.

3. This money should be designated and set aside for emergencies only. Many people practice what I call "put and take" savings, where they put money into a savings account every month because they know they should, only to end up taking it out by the end of the month to pay ordinary bills. Not only is this not an emergency fund, it's really not even savings because it's being consumed every month. Your emergency fund should be a "put and keep" type account where you add to it every month, and keep that money there for everything except a true emergency (unexpected loss of job, illness or injury that prevents work and incurs large bills, etc.)

4. Add to your emergency fund every month. Contributions to your emergency fund should be allocated in your monthly cash flow as a monthly fixed savings expense. Even after you've reached your emergency fund goal, continue to contribute, because any excess amount that you build up can be invested

or used to treat yourself to an unplanned vacation or other extravagance. The real benefit however, is that by continuing to contribute, you have already built into your cash flow a mechanism to rebuild this account after an unexpected emergency drains it.

5. Safety is the most important attribute of this money. Don't be tempted to risk that safety for a higher return. Many times the same economic downturn that causes someone to lose their job - and therefore have need for this money - is accompanied by a declining stock market. You'll designate other assets for higher returns, but this money must be kept safe. One strategy recommended by financial advisors is to "ladder" your emergency fund by putting one month's worth of expenses into six different 6-month CD's with a different one maturing each month. That way you'll always have money coming free and available without penalty each month if you need it, and you'll also be receiving slightly better returns on that money as compared to saving or checking accounts.

6. Finally, an emergency fund should not be considered the same as a transition fund if you are seeking a new career. If you are planning to make a career move and know that you will be interrupting your regular stream of income, save for that transition in addition to your emergency fund.

Protecting Yourself with Insurance

No one likes paying insurance premiums, but the protection it provides can often make the difference between achieving your dreams or not. Without proper insurance protection everything you accumulate on the upper levels of your pyramid can be wiped out with a single stroke of bad luck. But how much and what kinds of insurance should you have? The answer depends on your goals and situation.

Health Insurance

This one should be obvious, but I'll say it anyway - you need health insurance. How many people do you know who at some time in their life have suffered a major illness or injury? It's very likely that you yourself have. I was perfectly healthy (or so I thought) until my brain tumor was discovered. Yes, I've paid an awful lot in health insurance premiums over the years, but I'm guessing it still isn't close to what that surgery cost. Had I been forced to pay that on my own, it's likely I'd be bankrupt.

Health insurance, like all insurances, prevents against catastrophic financial loss. If you're lucky you'll never have to use it. But if you need it, it can preserve your financial assets so that when your body recovers, your balance sheet won't have to.

Life Insurance

Life insurance can be used for a number of estate planning purposes, but its primary goal is to protect your loved ones when you pass away. As such, all the exercises in regards to understanding your monthly cash flow relate directly back to how much life insurance you should have. Determining the full amount of life insurance you should carry will include:

1. A *final expenses fund* to cover funeral costs. These may run anywhere from $5,000 to $15,000.

2. An additional *emergency fund* to cover unexpected costs. When a loved one passes away, there may be many unexpected expenses. A relative may need help getting home for the funeral, fees may be incurred in re-arranging various accounts or assistance may need to be hired to arrange all of the affairs. Hopefully many of these will be covered in your other planning, but unexpected expenses do have a way of arising.

3. An *income replacement fund*. This is another reason why understanding your monthly cash flow statement is so important. The amount of insurance you need could vary widely based on whether you are a one- or two-income family, what your sources of income are (salary versus pension or Social Security), the amount you have already saved, or what your monthly expenses actually happen to be. While the conversation is a difficult one, it's important to look at all these factors and try to envision what the survivor's life would be like if one partner were gone. In a one-income family, would the surviving spouse have the ability to go back to work? Would they want to? In a two-income household would the survivor want - or need - to modify their work schedule in order to take care of young children? Would help need to be hired? What kind of Social Security benefits, if any, would the survivors be entitled to receive? How long would those benefits last? Would the survivor want to make any other significant life changes, like going back to school or starting a new career? All of these factors need to be examined to determine exactly how much monthly income will be needed and when it will be needed. In the next chapter, I'll share with you a formula to determine what lump sum dollar amount is needed to produce a specific amount of monthly income.

4. A *goal completion fund*. Like Emma, the client who opened her own art boutique in the years after her husband passed away, a goal completion fund allows our surviving family members to fulfill their lifelong dreams. It may include completing a college education fund for your children (or your spouse) or enough money to purchase that dream hideaway on the beach. Whatever the goals are that you identified in your cash flow savings budget, ask yourself if those goals are still relevant after you pass away. If for your survivors they are, then include those in your life insurance needs amount.

If one of your goals is to preserve your estate from estate taxes, life insurance in a properly titled trust can help you do that. With constantly changing estate tax laws however, these programs need to be reviewed at least every other year (preferably every year) to ensure that they continue to meet your goals. I suggest consulting with several qualified estate planning, insurance and financial planning professionals to find one you feel comfortable working with.

Disability Insurance

We typically insure those things that have value - our cars, our homes and our lives - just to name a few. But our greatest asset is our ability to earn an income. If indeed the financial independence that so many of us dream of is becoming harder and harder to achieve, then many of us will be forced to continue working well into our 60s and 70s. (Hopefully in a job we truly enjoy!) With that said however, our odds of suffering a disabling injury or illness are significantly higher than we might imagine. In any given year, one out of every eight people will suffer some kind of disability. A 30-year-old man has a one-in-five chance of suffering a long-term disability while a 30-year-old woman has a one-in-three chance. If you have not yet become financially independent and your standard of living is dependent on earning some type of wage, then you need disability insurance.

Long-Term Care Insurance

Most of us don't like the idea of going to a nursing home or even having the need for long-term care insurance, but if you're over age 55 you should definitely consider it. The average nursing home in the U.S. can cost over $74,000 per year, according to a 2009 survey by Genworth Financial. With an average stay length of two and a half years, that means the average stay in a U.S. nursing home can cost upwards of $185,000.

But why should someone in their mid-50s and in good health consider long-term care insurance? Because you're in your mid-50s and in good health. Like every other kind of insurance, long-term care is underwritten based on your age and health history, making it much more affordable for those who are younger and healthy. Once you reach age 60, the premium costs begin to rise dramatically. Most policies have a fixed-level premium that means once you get locked in, your individual rate cannot be changed, making it much more affordable to keep for the long term. Also, some policies these days are combining life and long-term care benefits ensuring that even if you don't ever use your policy, your beneficiaries will receive at least some benefit back from it.

Obviously there are other types of insurance that may be necessary, such as property and casualty to protect your car and home, liability insurance to protect against lawsuits or professional errors and omissions insurance to protect against accusations of professional incompetence. Depending on your situation, all of these should be examined to ensure you have protected all the areas that may be at risk. I know some of us may at times feel we are "insurance-poor," but as I've said, life has a way of throwing us curveballs. Insurance helps us manage those risks so we can continue on the path of our dreams.

Chapter 9

Climbing the Pyramid of Investments

Once we have the base of our pyramid covered by creating our balance sheet and cash flow statement, funding our emergency fund and covering our risks with insurance, we're finally ready to start accumulating wealth. In this chapter we'll cover the basics of investments.

The Basics

When it comes to investing, all investments can be categorized into two broad types - fixed investments or variable investments. In both cases the words fixed and variable refer to the principal amount of your investment - the money you have saved - but could equally apply to the money you earn on your principal. In a fixed-rate investment, your principal is guaranteed and will not fluctuate in value. If you put $10,000 into a fixed rate investment, your principal is guaranteed to remain at $10,000. The return *of* your principal is guaranteed. Things like savings accounts and CD's at a bank are examples of fixed rate investments.

Fixed-rate investments then pay interest - the return *on* your principal. Interest is the amount of money that the deposit institution will pay you for the use of your money. This concept is basic but important. The financial institution isn't going to pay you interest on your deposits out of the goodness of their hearts. They are paying you interest so that they can then turn around and loan that same money back out to others - maybe even to you - at a higher rate. The difference between what they pay you on your deposits and what they charge on loans is where they make their money. The advantages of a fixed-rate investment are that your principal is guaranteed, and you know exactly how much you are going to earn. The disadvantage is that you will earn a relatively low rate. The bank is only going to promise you a rate that they know they can safely beat.

Variable rate investments include things like stocks, bonds and mutual funds. In these types of investments your principal fluctuates, meaning you could put $10,000 into the investment and the next day it might be worth $5,000, $15,000 or anywhere in between (anywhere above or below for that matter as well!) In a variable-rate investment you have no guarantees as to how your money will perform. It may go up or down in value, and therefore the return both of and on your principal is unknown. The advantage to a variable-rate investment is that your investment has the *potential* to do better than a fixed rate, but it is not guaranteed. You are taking on the investment risk yourself, therefore the returns have the *possibility* of being higher, but again there is no guarantee. A comparison is shown in Table 9.1.

	Fixed	**Variable**
Principal Amount	Guaranteed	Fluctuates
Return on Principal	Known	Unknown
Examples	CDs, Savings Accounts	Stocks, Bonds, Mutual Funds
Long-term average return	3-5%	Varies, approximately 5-10%

Table 9.1
Comparison of Fixed and Variable-Rate Investments

Many of my clients found it helpful to imagine the investment world as a linear spectrum similar to the change continuum we talked about earlier. All of the fixed-rate investments basically anchor the left side of the investment risk spectrum. As you progress to the right the different types of investments continue to increase with greater risk as shown in Figure 9.2.

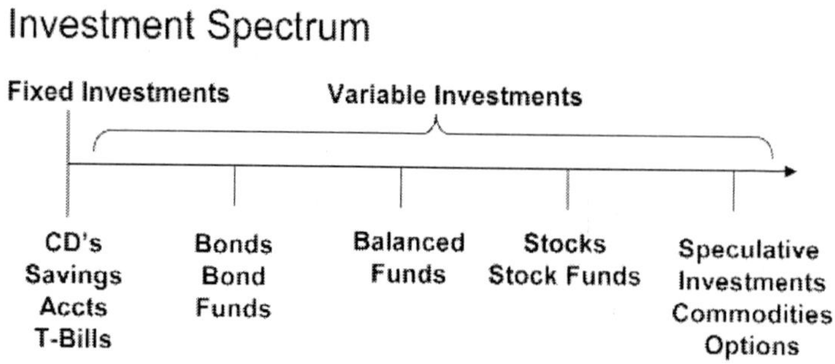

Figure 9.2
The Investment Spectrum

For purposes of our discussion here I am defining risk as the loss of principal. There are other types of risk, including inflation/purchasing power risk as we'll talk about in Chapter 10. But unless specified otherwise, we'll talk about risk as it relates to losing the principal amount that you have invested. As the wavy line in Figure 9.3 indicates, as you increase the amount of risk, the fluctuations to your principal also increase. For example, in any given year a $1,000 principal investment on the far left of the spectrum may fluctuate in value between $950 - $1,050, while one in the middle may fluctuate between $800 - $1, 200 and one on the far right may fluctuate from $0 - $2,000 or more. Take note of the low end of this last range. As the last few years have only too painfully taught us, the risk of losing a significant portion of your investment in any type of variable rate investment is very real. If the investment is truly speculative, your entire investment may very well be lost.

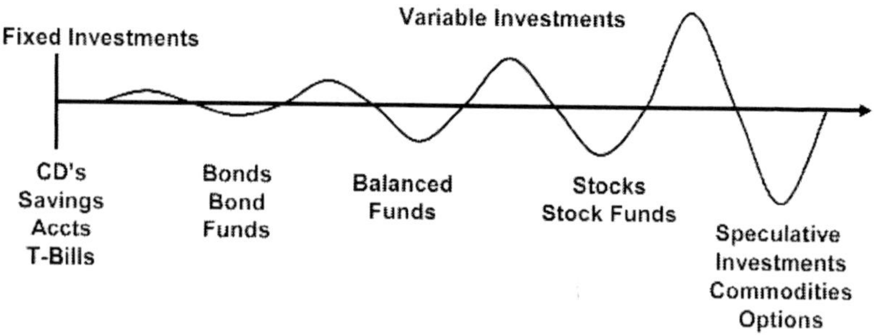

Figure 9.3
Volatility Increases with Risk

Why would someone take on this investment risk? Because of the magic of compound returns, which Albert Einstein once called "the most powerful force in the Universe." To understand compound returns, it's helpful to use the Rule of 72.

The Rule of 72 is a simple mathematical equation that tells us how long it will take to double our money at any given rate of return. It says that if you divide the rate of return into 72, the result will tell you the length of time it takes to double your money. For example, if you are receiving an 8% return, it will take 9 years to grow $1,000 into $2,000. (72 / 8% = 9 years). If you are receiving 6%, it will take 12 years to double your money. (72 / 6% = 12 years.) Obviously the higher return you receive, the less time it will take. When it comes to planning for retirement and our desire to grow our money as quickly as possible, the return we earn can have a significant impact. Let's look at an example.

Let's assume we have two 40-year-old individuals, Investor A and Investor B, who both have $25,000 to invest. Let's further assume that Investor A chooses a relatively low-risk investment paying 4%, while Investor B chooses a higher-risk investment that while not guaranteed, over the long-term earns 8%. Using our rule of 72, Investor A will double his money every 18 years, while Investor B will double his in 9 years. Over time the growth of the accounts will look like this.

Age	40	49	58	67	76
A - 4%	$25,000		$50,000		$100,000
B - 8%	$25,000	$50,000	$100,000	$200,000	$400,000

Table 9.4
The Effects of the Rule of 72

As you can see, the higher rate of return makes a huge difference in the amount of money a person can accumulate over time. With just two additional "doubles," Investor B was able to accumulate four times as much as investor A. The more "doubles" you can get, the bigger difference it will make. As we saw in Chapter 3 with the example of doubling a penny everyday for 30 days, no one gets too excited about turning $1,000 into $2,000 or $2,000 into $4,000. But if I can turn $100,000 into $200,000 or $200,000 into $400,000, now you've got my attention! That's why we're willing to take on higher risk.

Now that we know the risks and the rewards of basic investing, let's look at some specific investment vehicles.

Short-Term Investments: CDs, Savings Accounts and T-Bills

Short-term investments, our first investment level of the financial planning pyramid, are primarily fixed-rate investments sometimes referred to as *cash equivalents* and include savings accounts, CDs and Treasury bills. Savings accounts, as you probably know, are nothing more than deposit accounts at a bank or credit union. Your money is immediately liquid (available to you) should you want to withdraw it, and is guaranteed by both the financial institution and, up to certain dollar amounts - $250,000 until 2013 - by the federal government. As such, a savings account pays very little interest, which raises an important point.

There are three qualities that we all want that can be associated with any investment - safety, liquidity and the *potential* for a higher return. Unfortunately, any investment can provide only two of these three with absolute certainty. There is no investment that is completely safe, completely liquid, and provides a definite or even potential high return. (If someone offers you an investment that promises all three, don't walk, *run* away.) Therefore in the case of a savings account, you receive safety and liquidity but a very low return.

In the case of a certificate of deposit (CD) you are essentially promising to leave your money with the financial institution for some length of time, thereby agreeing to limit your own access to your money. In return for giving up some of this liquidity, the bank pays a slightly higher interest rate. Now you've got safety and a slightly higher return, but you've sacrificed some liquidity. Again, any investment will allow you only two of the three qualities we all want.

There are some investments that attempt to balance the three. But remember, any investment that attempts to balance safety, liquidity and a high return, is compromising at least one of these to some degree. If it's completely safe and completely liquid, it won't provide much of a return. If it's completely safe and has a good return, it's probably not liquid without a penalty. (Meaning that like a CD, you have to leave it there for some period of time. If you attempt to take your money out before that time period is up, there is usually a penalty for early withdrawal.) If it's liquid and has a good *potential* return, it carries some risk of losing some portion of your principal.

The currently recognized world standard as the ultimate in safe, risk-free investments remains the U.S. Treasury bill (T-bill). A T-bill is a short-term loan to and backed by the "full faith and credit" of the U.S. government. We often tend to think negatively of the U.S. government and wonder how long it can stay in business, but the reality is the U.S. government is the most stable organization on earth. It has the ability to tax its citizens to repay its debt obligations and, even though some may argue the U.S is losing its world economic leadership position to China, is still considered the safest place in the world to invest.

Intermediate-Term Investments: Bonds

As we move one step up the investment spectrum, the first real investment we get to is bonds. A bond is nothing more than a loan. When you purchase a bond, you become the lender, essentially loaning your money to whatever organization is issuing the bond. Just like when you borrow money, a bond carries specific terms. When you borrow money, the bank charges you a very specific interest rate. A bond does the same thing in that it pays a specified interest rate. When you borrow money, the bank also sets the terms regarding when the money will be repaid. A bond does the same thing in that it carries a maturity date. The only real difference between a loan that you take out from a bank and bond is in how the payments are made. Typically when you borrow money, your payments include both interest and principal. A bond typically pays only the interest over the life of the bond, with a balloon payment returning your entire principal in one lump sum at the end of the bond's term (called the maturity date.)

All kinds of organizations issue bonds, from the U.S. government, to city, state and other municipal entities, as well as businesses and corporations traded on the various stock exchanges. All of them have the need to borrow money from time to time, and the reality is that often the amounts they need to borrow are so large that no bank is willing or able to lend that much at a rate the borrower can afford to pay. Hence, they spread out the loan by issuing bonds, thereby borrowing money from thousands of people or organizations in much smaller amounts.

Let's use the common example of a local school district that wants to build a new school building. A school district seldom has the money on hand to build the school, so it needs to borrow the money. Since the district is a local tax-supported entity, unlike a typical business it can't simply go to a bank and ask for a loan, so it issues bonds. By issuing these bonds with the help of an investment bank, the district raises the money it needs to build the school.

From the bond buyers (i.e. you, the investor's) perspective, the question becomes, "Where is the school district going to come up with the money to repay these bonds?" The answer is from the property owners in the school district. Before the school district can issue the bonds, it needs to get approval from the property owners in the district. An election is held where a school bond measure is put on the ballot asking the property owners if they are willing to have their property taxes raised to repay the bonds that will be used to build the new school. If the voters approve the measure, the bonds are issued and the school is built.

For the U.S. government, other municipalities and corporations, bonds offer a great way to borrow money to fund projects that would otherwise be cost prohibitive.

To truly understand bonds, however we need to look a little deeper. The first thing we need to look at is called credit risk. Since investing in a bond means you are lending your money to some organization, you are probably going to be concerned about that organization's ability to repay the money you've lent to them. Just like when you borrow money, the bank asks for your income and debt information to assess your ability to repay the loan. In the same way, you should be concerned about the bond issuer's ability to repay the interest and principal on the money you lend to them through the purchase of their bonds. Think about it - would you rather lend money to the U.S. government or to Joe's Corner Garage Bike Shop? Which do you think has the greater ability to repay you?

Thankfully there are ratings agencies such as Standard & Poor's, Moody's and the A.M. Best Company that are experts in determining a bond issuer's ability to repay. "Experts," however, is a relative term. These organizations are certainly better than any of us who do not have access to the same information or the knowledge to interpret that information, but as the economic crisis of 2008-2009 proved, a high rating by any of the various agencies does not guarantee the issuer's ability to repay.

Each of the rating agencies has its own scale on which they rate bond issuers according to their "creditworthiness" - their ability to repay those bonds. Fortunately the scales they use are reasonably similar so it is not difficult to compare one agency's rating of a particular bond issuer to another's. Table 9.5 shows the rating tiers for both Moody's and Standard & Poor's and what some of the ratings mean.

Moody's	Standard & Poor's	Description
Aaa	AAA	Credit risk is almost zero. An issuer with this rating has extremely strong capacity to meet its financial commitments. There is almost no risk that the issuer will not be able to repay the bond.
Aa	AA	Safe investment. There is very low risk of failure or issuer's ability to repay.
A-1, A	A	An issuer rated 'A' has strong capacity to meet its financial commitments but is somewhat more susceptible to the adverse effects of changes in circumstances and economic conditions than issuers in higher-rated categories.
Baa-1, Baa	BBB	Medium safe investment. An issuer rated 'BBB' has adequate capacity to meet its financial commitments but adverse economic conditions may weaken its capacity to continue to meet its obligations.
Ba	BB	Speculative investment. The issuer faces major ongoing uncertainties and exposure to adverse business, financial, or economic conditions that could lead to an inability to repay its bond obligations.
B, Caa	B, CCC,CC	Speculative to highly speculative investment. The issuer currently has the ability to repay its bond obligations, but existing conditions may impair their willingness or ability to continue. The issuer may also be dependent on favorable economic circumstances to continue to meet its obligations.
CA, C	D	The issuer is likely to default on its bond obligations.
NR		Not rated.

Table 9.5
Bond Issuer Creditworthiness Rating Scales

Note that a rating of "NR - Not Rated" is not a bad rating, it simply means the issuer has not hired the agency to conduct an analysis and provide a rating. As the cost for this service can be substantial, many municipalities choose not to incur that cost and simply issue the bonds based on their past history. For a municipality you are familiar and comfortable with, this may be acceptable. But for an area of the country that you are unfamiliar with, you may want to familiarize yourself with the economy in those areas before purchasing unrated bonds from those municipalities.

If all things were equal, we would always purchase just the highest-rated bonds, right? The reality is that all things are not equal. Bond issuers are very concerned about the rating they receive from the various agencies as the rating directly impacts how much interest they have to pay on their bonds.

Going back to our previous example, if both Joe's Corner Garage Bike Shop (rated BBB) and the U.S. government (technically not rated, but deemed equivalent to AAA) were going to pay 5%, you would always choose the one with less risk, in this case the U.S. government bond. Therefore, in order to entice you to purchase their bonds and loan them your money, Joe's Corner Garage Bike Shop is forced to increase the interest rate it is willing to pay. If Joe's decides to pay 6%, then you as an investor are forced to make a decision - are you willing to take the extra risk of investing with Joe in order to receive a higher return on your money?

This increased risk/return pattern continues all the way down the ratings spectrum. Bonds rated BBB and above are considered high-quality, "investment grade" bonds. As the credit quality of the issuer gets lower and lower, the interest they need to pay to entice borrowers to invest with them becomes higher and higher. Once you go below a rating of BBB, the bonds become what are now known as "high-yield" bonds. Because the creditworthiness of the issuers is considered high risk or speculative, the issuers are forced to offer high interest rates, (i.e. yields) on their bonds. Today the term "high-yield" is used to put a positive spin on these higher-risk bonds. Back in the 1980s these same low-rated bonds were known as junk bonds, and were all the rage until a small recession in 1990 caused the collapse of the junk bond market and millions lost their life savings.

The issuer's creditworthiness is not the only factor that impacts the amount of interest a bond will pay. The length of time, or how long the organization wants to borrow your money, also impacts the rate of interest a bond will pay. Logically, shorter-term bonds pay lower rates and longer-term bonds pay higher rates. If someone asks you to loan them some money but promises to pay you back tomorrow, you probably won't even bother to charge them interest. (That's assuming you know them, trust them, and decide to lend it to them in the first place.) On the other hand, if they ask you to lend them that money for five years, now you have to think about what else you could do with that money. At the very least you could put it in a savings account and earn some small amount of interest on it. To be willing to lend that money for longer lengths of time, the issuer needs to pay you more. The relationship between interest rates and time are shown by a graph called the yield curve, illustrated in Figure 9.6 below.

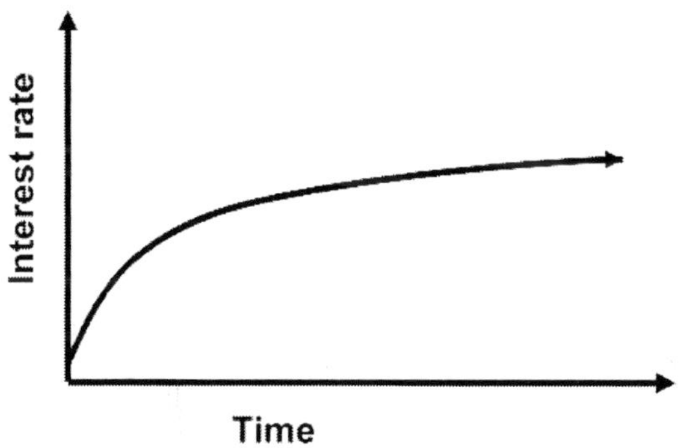

Figure 9.6
The Yield Curve

The difference between U.S. T-bills, notes and bonds is simply the length of time to maturity. All are obligations of the U.S. government, but T-bills are loans that will mature in one year or less. Treasury notes come in terms of 2 - 10 years, while Treasury bonds are issued for 30 years.

Let's say then you purchased a 30-year Treasury bond backed by the full faith and credit of the United States government. You're receiving a reasonably good long-term interest rate because you purchased a long-term bond, and your money is safe because you purchased it from the most secure borrower in the world. As long as you hold the bond until it matures, you'll get all of your money back, plus 30 years worth of interest along the way. All is good, right?

It is if you don't need your money back before the bond matures, but thirty years is a long time. What if you need your money before then? This is a good news/bad news situation. The good news is that you can sell your bond before it matures; the bad news is you may not get 100% of your money back when you do. Here's how it works.

Interest rates are changing all the time. The Federal Reserve Board (the Fed) adjusts the interest rates that it charges to the nation's banks in hopes of maintaining a robust but not overheated economy. In tough economic times the Fed lowers interest rates to encourage economic activity through borrowing and spending. In strong economic times the Fed increases interest rates to slow down growth and prevent inflation.

As interest rates change, the principal value of existing bonds is affected as new bonds with new rates become available. Let's say for example that your 30-year U.S. Treasury bond pays 5%, but because the economy (in this example) is good, the Fed decides to increase interest rates so that new 30-year bonds now pay 6%. If someone new enters the market looking to purchase a 30-year treasury bond, whose are they going to buy? Yours, paying 5%, or a new one paying 6%? If you really wanted to unload your bond, you would be forced to reduce the price to make it comparable to the new bond paying 6%. Because interest rates went up, the value of your bond went down. It doesn't matter if you have a AAA-rated bond or a BBB-rated bond, when interest rates move, bond values change also.

The good news is that the inverse of this is true also. If the Fed lowered interest rates and new bonds were now paying only 4%, your bond would become more valuable and the price of your bond would increase. This relationship between interest rates and bond prices is known as interest rate risk and is shown in Figure 9.7.

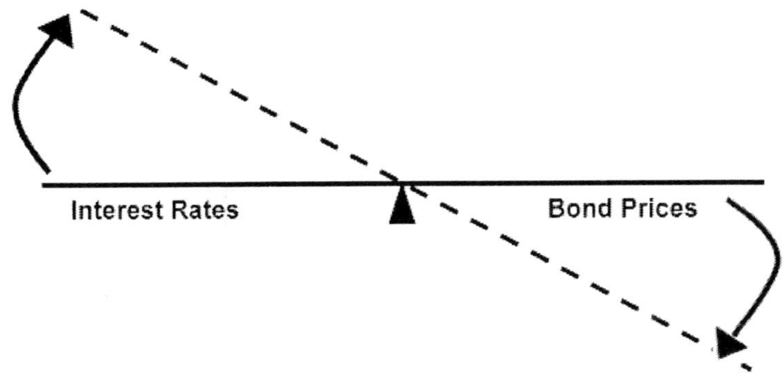

Figure 9.7
The Effect of Interest Rates on Bond Prices

The relationship between bond prices and interest rates is often illustrated as an old-fashioned see-saw. As one goes up, the other goes down. As you can see, there is a direct but inverse relationship between the two that works both ways. When interest rates go down, the prices and value of existing bonds goes up. Obviously the amount of change in interest rates will also factor in. A small change in interest rates will result in only a small change in prices. Larger changes in interest rates produce larger price swings.

This see-saw analogy is also good for making one additional point about the *amount* of change that various bonds experience. First, consider the fulcrum in the center to represent the maturity date of your bonds. Next, consider the line that extends to the right to be a timeline, ranging from just a few months right next to the fulcrum extending out to 30 years at the far end of the line. The amount of price movement of any bond is directly related to the distance or length of time away from the maturity date. The longer the length of time to maturity the more price volatility the bond will experience. If for example, interest rates were to move by 1% (which would be considered a huge move at any one time) then a bond with 30 years to maturity might experience a full 10% change in value. A $1,000 30-year bond might now be worth anywhere from $900 (if the interest rate move were 1% up) to $1,100 (if the interest rate move were 1% down.) At the same time however, a $1,000 bond with only 1 year to maturity might see its price fluctuate from $995 - $1,005 as a result of the same 1% change in interest rates. You can see in Figure 9.8 that those bonds with shorter terms experience less volatility and less price movement compared to those on the longer end of the scale. Again, this makes sense when you consider the real-life application. The issuer has promised to repay the 100% full face value of the bond at maturity. As the timeframe of a bond gets closer to its maturity date, its price will automatically begin to approach its face value.

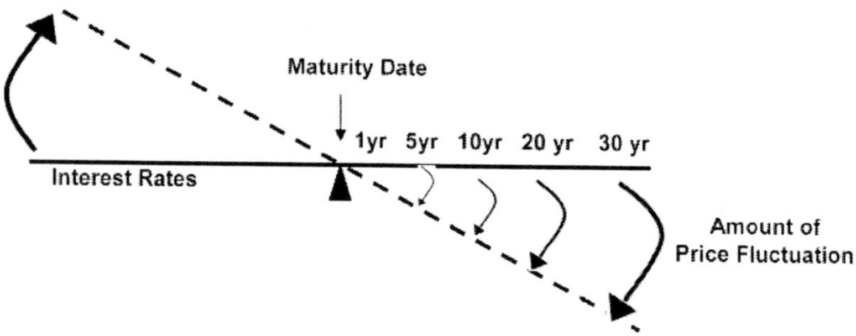

Figure 9.8
The Impact of Interest Rates and Time on Bond Prices

It's this combination of price volatility and fixed characteristics that create much of the confusion about bonds. Because they pay a specified interest and are worth a guaranteed face value at maturity, bonds are often referred to as "fixed income" investments. That phrase however, often leads people to believe they cannot ever lose money by investing in a bond. As we've just seen, that is obviously not the case. Equally clear however, is that because bonds do have a promised, known value at some date in the future, they are considerably safer than stocks, which offer no such promises.

Long Term Investments: Stocks

Unlike bonds where you simply loan your money to a government or business and expect a repayment of your principal and interest, when you invest in a stock, you are becoming an owner of that company, with all the risks and rewards that come with it. The risk of course is that there is no promise of any particular return on your money or even of your money. If the company behind the stock you own goes out of business, you could lose your entire investment. On the other hand, if the company discovers a cure for cancer or becomes the next Microsoft, you stand to do very well. Trying to figure out which is which is the trick. While analyzing stocks to try to guess how well any one might do is extremely difficult, understanding them is actually much easier. Even so, to truly understand some of the implications of investing in stocks, we need to have a solid understanding of the basics, so that's where we'll begin.

Just like people, all companies go through a life cycle as shown in Figure 9.9.

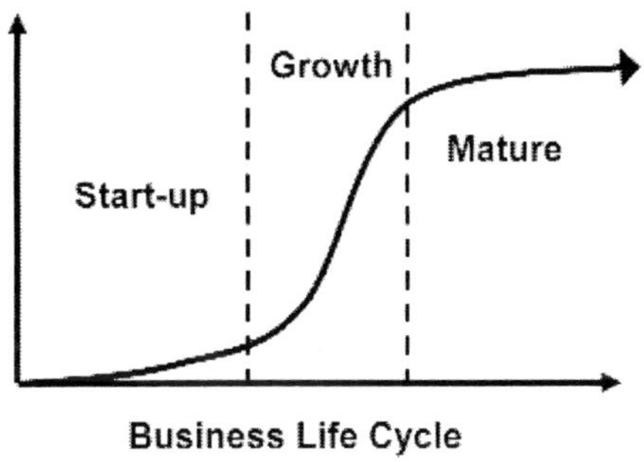

Figure 9.9
The Business Life Cycle

When a business is begun, it is often done on a shoestring budget with limited resources. One of the best examples of this is when Bill Hewlett and Dave Packard formed Hewlett-Packard Company in 1939 inside an old garage in Palo Alto, CA with initial working capital of $538. Today HP employs over 300,000 people around the world with over $100 billion in revenue. As the business grows, additional capital is often needed to expand capacity. While the business could issue bonds to raise the needed capital, bonds as we know, need to be repaid, which creates a financial obligation that may actually impede the growth they seek. Another option is to "go public" by offering ownership shares of the company in the form of stock. When a company first goes public, its stock is offered for sale in an initial public offering (IPO). It should be noted that the only time the company actually receives any of the money that investors pay when purchasing the stock is during this initial public offering. Any transactions in the stock after that occur between existing shareholders in what is called the secondary market. This will be important when we talk about investor behavior in a few moments.

With this new infusion of capital from the IPO, the company is now in a position to significantly grow its business. The company then enters the growth phase of its life cycle and may stay there for several years or even decades. During this time, new products are developed, new markets are opened and the company focuses on continued growth. As such, any profits that the company earns are typically plowed back into the company for additional research and development of new products and expanding markets.

Eventually however, the growth will begin to flatten out and the cash flow will stabilize to the point where the company will begin to distribute some of those earning out to the owners of the company - the stock shareholders - in the form of dividends. At this point the company has entered the mature phase of its lifecycle and will likely stay there for many years or decades until it goes out of business or is sold or absorbed into another company.

This background is important because like bonds, different types of stocks have different risk-and-reward characteristics. Stocks of companies that are in their start-up phase or have just come out of their IPO are typically much more volatile - meaning their prices will jump around more - than stocks of mature companies that have been traded for years. Although make no mistake, stocks of all companies, as we've seen in the last couple of years, can be very volatile. Figure 9.10 shows where stocks in different stages of the business lifecycle will fall on the investment spectrum.

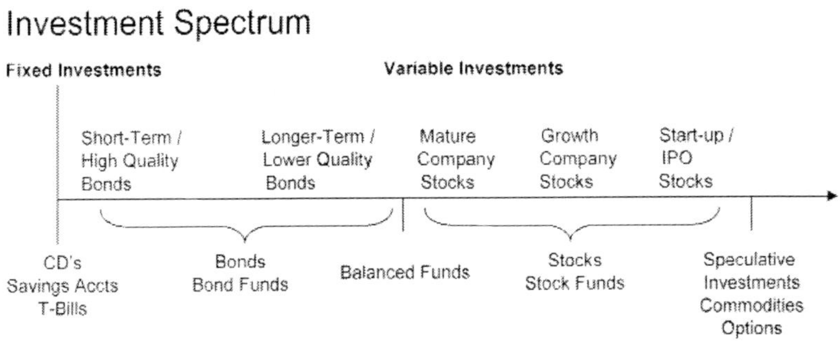

Figure 9.10
The Investment Spectrum

There has been and continues to be a lot of debate over which type of stock is better to invest in - growth stocks or mature stocks, which are often referred to as value stocks. (The full definition of a value stock includes much more than its phase in the business life cycle, but for now this limited definition will suffice.) Just by looking at the rapid expansion that occurs during the growth phase of the business lifecycle graph, you would think that growth stocks would do much better than value/mature stocks, but that is not always the case.

One problem with growth stocks is that they are often doing business in rapidly developing industries with rapidly evolving technologies. A company that appears to be on the cusp of becoming mainstream may be quickly displaced by a new company with a more user-friendly product. For each Microsoft that acquires a significant market share and goes on to become a mature company, there are literally dozens of others that fade away after failing to reach that critical mass. Hundreds of companies die off before they can reach that mature company phase. By continuing to invest in growth companies, we are bound to get some losers from time to time. At some point, those losses more than offset the winners, and we reach a point of diminishing returns. Beyond that point the additional risk we take outweighs the rewards for taking that risk, and our returns begin to suffer. While there will always be periods when growth investing outperforms value investing, historically it has been better to back off the risk a bit. Between 1927 and 2006 large U.S. value stocks averaged a return of 11.6% per year, while growth stocks over the same period averaged 9.4%.[6]

This desire to find the next huge stock winner leads a lot of people to do more than just invest in the stock market, they speculate in the market, meaning they are not necessarily looking for the next great company, but rather the next great stock. Speculators don't care if the company has a sound business model or will ever reach the mature stage, they're just looking for great stories - stocks that will make big moves either up or down. This speculation, to the dismay of long-term investors, causes a lot of volatility in the markets.

As we said a moment ago, after the IPO all transactions in any particular stock occur between individual investors in the secondary market. This secondary market consists of all the physical and electronic stock exchanges around the world including the New York Stock Exchange, NASDAQ and the less-often referenced American Stock Exchange, just to name a few. For years the financial services industry has held onto the belief that these investors who trade shares back and forth act rationally when making their buy and sell decisions. The theory, called the Efficient Market Hypothesis (EMH), states that the price of a stock at any given moment represents a logical evaluation of the known information that might impact the future value of the company. Further, EMH states that stock share prices are priced efficiently, which is to say that they accurately represent that future value at any given moment.

If that is true, how then does one explain either the wild sell-off in stock prices that were seen both following the 9/11 attacks in 2001 and the financial crisis in 2008, or the massive run-up in prices that led to the technology bubble in 1999-2000 or the spike in oil prices in 2008? A second theory, known as behavioral finance, asserts that the financial markets are not rational at all, but are prone to periods of irrational behavior based primarily on the emotions of greed and fear. According to behavioral finance advocates, investors will act rationally as long as there are no emotional triggers in play. As soon as some news or personal event triggers an emotion - which is to say most of the time - those emotions override logical reasoning and cause investors to behave irrationally.

[6] http://ifa.com

One of our biggest mistakes, according to behavioral finance theory, is our inability to anticipate changes. When we see the market heading in one direction, we tend to assume it will continue in that direction. During the technology bubble of the late 90s, small start-up companies were rushing to go public as investors bid up the prices of just about any company that included the phrase "dot-com" in its name. Many of these companies had no business model, no infrastructure and no rational way to support their stratospheric stock prices. And yet investors, driven by both the greed of getting rich quickly and the fear of being left behind, believed that these rising prices would continue. We failed to anticipate a time when the greed of speculation would give way to the rationalization that these companies did not warrant those high valuations and that the direction of stock prices would change as a result.

This inability to anticipate changes works in the other direction as well. During the panic of late 2008 investors continued to dump stocks of financially healthy companies out of fear that those declining prices would eventually erode to zero. At the time it didn't matter if the company was financially healthy or not, the good stocks were sold along with the bad.

The implications of this inconsistent behavior pose a real problem for both investors and financial advisors. Financial professionals are taught that the markets are efficient and rational, and therefore often adopt a "buy and hold" strategy for their clients, advising that investors should just ride out the volatility. The problem is that those who abide by that strategy are taken along for the ride by those who are reacting emotionally. It's like standing in the face of an oncoming storm. Eventually the storm will pass, but when it does the damage is often already done. We'll talk more about investment strategies and how an investor might deal with this irrational behavior a bit later on.

Packaged Products - Mutual Funds, UITs and ETFs

Your mother always said, "Don't put all your eggs in one basket." When it comes to investing, the investments you can use to follow your mother's advice include mutual funds, Unit Investment Trusts (UITs) and Exchange Traded Funds (ETFs).

Mutual Funds

A mutual fund is nothing more than a package of other stocks and or bonds. Rather than investing in a single stock or a single bond, a mutual fund pools your money with other investors, hires a professional money manager and diversifies your investment by spreading it out through the purchase of literally hundreds of different stocks or bonds. There are several advantages to investing this way:

1. It's more affordable. Individual stocks still tend to trade in "round lots" of 100 shares per transaction. If you're looking at a stock that's priced at $50 per share, that means you need $5,000 (plus transaction costs) just to buy one round lot. Most of us would have to save up for several months or years before we came up with enough just to make one investment. A mutual fund allows you to invest as little as $25 per month, making them much more accessible to the average investor.

2. It's more liquid. Let's say you invested $10,000 into a single bond but unexpectedly needed $2,000 back out. If your investment were just that $10,000 bond, you would have to sell the whole bond just to get your $2,000. With a mutual fund you can sell any dollar amount when you need it.

3. It's more diversified. Even if you have $10,000 to invest, if the individual stocks you want run $50 per share each, that means you could buy two different stocks. You had better choose wisely because your investment is riding on just the performance of those two companies. In a mutual fund, your money is pooled with other investors, allowing it to be spread

out over hundreds of different stocks or bonds. This diversification does not protect against a loss or assure a gain, but it does tend to "average out" the winners and the losers producing relatively less volatility than individual stocks or bonds.

4. It's actively, professionally managed. I know, especially after 2008-2009 a lot of folks are questioning the value of their professional managers. But if the professionals who have the time, knowledge and access to information that most of us don't are having a difficult time, how do you think you would do? The very fact that the day-trading craze of the late 90s has all but disappeared in the aftermath of these two market downturns in 2000-02 and 2008-09 is testament to the difficulty in picking individual stocks.

5. It allows you to invest exactly to your risk comfort level. Mutual funds are like Baskin-Robbins - a flavor for everyone all the way up and down the investment spectrum. If you want to stay at the low end of the investment spectrum but want something with the potential for a better return than a CD, you can invest in a mutual fund that buys nothing but short-term, high-quality bonds. If you want something more aggressive, you can invest in a fund that purchases nothing but growth stocks. If you are somewhere in the middle, you can purchase what is called a "Balanced Fund" that invests in both stocks and bonds. The fact is you can invest in almost anything - stocks, bonds, gold, real estate, currencies, foreign stocks, foreign bonds and more - through mutual funds.

Mutual funds are far from a perfect investment, however. They have a couple of disadvantages as well:

1. They are still variable-rate investments and will fluctuate in value. Some people mistakenly believe that because mutual funds are so diversified, or

because they are commonly offered inside their employers' 401(k) plan, that they can't lose money in a mutual fund. Even mutual funds that invest in the lowest risk bonds still pose the risk of some loss of principal.

2. They charge fees. All funds charge fees of one kind or another. All of them. 100%. Even those that are "no-load." Part of that fee goes to the professional management of the fund (the management fee), and other parts go to pay the advisor who helps you select which type of fund is best for you (the load). All of these fees may be very well justified based on the performance of the fund and the service/assistance you receive from your advisor, or not justified at all if the performance or service is lacking.

Unit Investment Trusts and Exchange Traded Funds

UITs are similar to mutual funds in that they diversify your investment, but they differ in the fact that they are not managed. Over the life of a mutual fund the manager is constantly purchasing and selling individual stocks or bonds within the fund in an effort to maximize the return. With a UIT, once the securities are selected, those securities stay in the UIT until they mature (as is the case with bonds) and no other new securities are added.

An ETF is also similar to a mutual fund, but also has some important differences. First, an ETF always mirrors an index. An index is a group of stocks or bonds that have been pre-selected to statistically measure some segment of the market such as financial services, health care or long-term corporate bonds. The most well-known indices are the Dow Jones Industrial Average (the Dow) and the Standard & Poor's (S&P) 500. The Dow measures the performance of 30 actively-traded, primarily industrial stocks, while the S&P 500 is a broader indicator of 500 companies believed to be more representative of the market as a whole. There are literally hundreds of indices out there that measure all kinds of different segments in the market.

These indices have become the benchmarks by which active mutual fund managers are measured. If a fund is performing better than its corresponding index, then its manager is felt to be adding value and earning the management fee that the fund charges. Unfortunately many funds - sometimes two out of three - often fail to beat their comparable index. That statistic has caused many investors to wonder why they were paying management fees. Since there is no way to invest in the index itself, ETFs were created and have subsequently boomed in popularity as a way for investors to receive close to market-equivalent performance with fewer fees.

A second major difference between ETFs and mutual funds is that ETFs trade throughout the day like stocks, whereas most mutual fund prices are calculated only once per day to reflect the closing prices of each of the stocks within the fund. As a result, ETF shareholders are able to react to market conditions throughout the day, while mutual fund shareholders must wait until the market closes to buy or sell their shares.

Investment Timeframes

Now that we know what each of these different types of investments are, how does that relate back to our short-, intermediate- and long-term investment levels on our financial planning pyramid? In the case of investing, those expressions – short, intermediate and long term - are defined differently than they are for your debts on your personal balance sheet. When it comes to investing, the basic rule of thumb is this: The longer your investment timeframe, the more risk you can afford to take with your investments.

Money that is used for your monthly cash flow to pay the bills and buy the groceries is kept in a low-risk savings or checking account. Your emergency fund, while it may sit there for several years if no emergency arises, still needs to be kept safe and liquid *in case* you need it on a moment's notice. Money that you'll use to pay next year's school tuition, buy a new car within two years, or put a down payment on a house within three years, should also be kept in very low-risk, relatively safe investments such as the CDs, savings accounts or perhaps a money-market mutual fund. These short-term investments are the vehicles to use for any money that you anticipate needing within the next three years.

That said, many of us in our 40s and 50s may be taking time to "re-career" by going back to school to re-train ourselves into a career that is more personally meaningful. If that schooling is expected to take two to three years and you plan on living off your savings during that time, that savings should be kept in very short-term, safe investments so there is no risk of losing the money you'll be depending on.

If you have intermediate-term goals of say four to seven years, bonds, bond mutual funds and bond-based ETFs are good investments for that time frame. These might include college education funds for your middle-school age children or a portion of your retirement savings if retirement is within that time frame. The key here is that while you can afford to see some fluctuation in your principal, you can't afford to see a lot. If your goals are on the long end of that timeframe, you might even consider a balanced mutual fund or balanced portfolio of ETFs, but you would want to adjust that portfolio regularly to become more conservative as the time frame for needing that money draws nearer. Regardless of what your goals may be, we would classify them as intermediate term if they were four to seven years out. Some variations of a bond-based investment would likely be appropriate for that length of time.

Stocks and stock-based mutual funds, ETFs and UITs are only appropriate for long-term investments when your goals are at least eight to ten years out or more. When it comes to retirement accounts, we need to remember that we're investing not just up until our retirement date, but that we are likely to live another 20 or 30 years into retirement. Therefore a portion of our retirement accounts, even at retirement, should be invested for some kind of long-term growth.

In the next chapter, we'll begin to look at strategies how to balance our expenses with the amount of income we can reasonably expect from our investments.

Chapter 10

Two Sides of the Equation

Now that you have pretty good idea of what your ideal life looks like and a basic idea of the financial tools available to help get you there, how do you develop the strategies to move from where you are today to where you want to be? The first step is to figure out your number.

What is Your Number?

Like so many things in the world of financial planning, there are both sophisticated financial planning programs available to help you determine how much you need to become financially independent and retire, and there are rules of thumb that provide general guidance. While most financial planning software creates some very impressive reports, the reality is that all those facts and figures are based on a set of assumptions that may or may not come true. Financial Eagles will often painstakingly research and investigate all the variables to ensure they are getting the most accurate estimate possible. They'll pore over reams of inflation data (as one example) in an attempt to determine the exact, precise number to apply to the program. The problem is that there's no way of knowing if the future will bear that number out. With so many variables, a mistaken assumption in any one can create a projection that is drastically different than your future reality. That said, when it comes to determining your "number," a good rule of thumb often provides as accurate a picture as the most sophisticated software. In either case, it's important to understand what those variables are, so let's take a look at just a few.

The first variable we need to guesstimate is how long you're going to live. Since no one really knows the answer to that question, it's helpful to look at actuarial statistics. Again, someone who is age 65 today is expected on average to reach age 83. But probably more important is that there is close to a 50% chance that one member of a married couple age 65 today will live to be at least 90 years old, and an 18% chance of one of them making it to age 95. Since outliving our assets is one of our greatest retirement fears as we grow older, most prudent retirement plans include a life expectancy to at least age 90, often even to 95.

The second variable we need to determine is how much income you'll need when you retire. There are two methods to determine this. The first and easiest way is to use a percentage of your pre-retirement income. Many financial advisors or retirement calculator web sites suggest using approximately 80% of your pre-retirement income as a good baseline goal of what your retirement income needs will be. While this may turn out well for some, it often doesn't take into account the specific priorities and life goals that you may have for your retirement. Do you want to travel? Start a business? Develop a hobby? What is it that you really want to do with the second half of your life, and how much money will it take to do it in the lifestyle that you want? Simply using a round number, whether it's 80% or 200% of your pre-retirement income, doesn't assure you of having the resources you need to do exactly what you want.

A second, more precise method is to determine your retirement income needs based on what your current lifestyle expenses are now, and then make adjustments based on your known goals and priorities. The personal cash flow statement introduced earlier is a great tool for this. By tracking your current monthly expenses, you begin to understand exactly how you spend your money. Is your spending aligned with your goals and priorities? Are there "leaks" in your monthly cash flow where you spend money but receive virtually no appreciable lifestyle benefit? Are there expenses that you have now, like a car loan, credit card or second mortgage payment that will be paid off and therefore no longer be needed when you retire? Are there other expenses, like a travel budget, a start-up business expense, or health care expenses that will need to be added? By clearly defining your priorities and getting a good handle on what you want to do when you retire - and what it will cost to do it - you can define a "number" that you can feel confident about.

Once you determine how much monthly income you'll need in today's dollars, you need to apply the third variable - inflation. How much money will it take 25 years from now to maintain the same standard of living you have today? Over the past 100 years, inflation in the U.S. has ranged from as low as -2% to as high as +14%, but has seemed to average around 3.5%. What that means is that every 20 or so years, the cost of living will double. If it takes $50,000 to maintain your standard of living today, it will take $100,000 to maintain the same standard of living 20 years from now, and $200,000 to maintain that standard 40 years from now.

It's that constant erosion of our purchasing power that makes the fourth variable - our investment return - so important. While many of us would prefer not to deal with the ups and downs of the stock market, we also don't want to live on a fixed income. Creating an investment portfolio that provides enough growth to keep pace with inflation while maintaining the security of our principal is no easy task. Since safer investments such as CDs, money markets and T-bills often fail to keep pace with inflation, we're forced to consider investments that carry at least some risk. But as we've seen over the last decade, even small amounts of risk can sometimes lead to disastrous results.

While it is easy enough to estimate an answer for each of these variables, the fact is each remains just an estimate. If we plan to live to age 95, but in fact live to be 105, our plan may well fail us in the final years of our life. If we fail to anticipate some unexpected expense, a sudden rise in inflation or a down year or two in the stock market, our best laid plans may fail. That is not to say we should take the full Condor view and simply give up or say "why bother?" The fact is we owe it to ourselves to take on the characteristics of the Eagle and do as much planning as we reasonably can. But even that will not provide a 100% guarantee. At some point we simply have to trust that we've done as much as we can.

So while there are times - like when determining how much income you'll need at retirement - that using exact precise numbers are essential, the truth is that in determining your probability of success, a good rule of thumb provides as valid an answer as some of the most sophisticated software. In the case of planning for retirement, here is the rule of thumb I recommend.

> *For every $1,000 of monthly income that you feel you need that WON'T be covered by a cost-of-living adjusted pension or Social Security, you need to have saved $300,000 in savings and investments.*

The basis behind this 300:1 ratio is fairly simple. Forget for a moment what kind of return you think you can earn on your $300,000 investment, but think instead about how much you will withdraw from it. My experience as well as extensive research conducted to determine the optimal safe withdrawal rate from any portfolio has shown that a withdrawal rate of 4% is considered to be safely sustainable. A 4% withdrawal from $300,000 equals an annual distribution of $12,000 per year, or $1,000 per month. Hence, for every $1,000 of monthly income you need, you should have $300,000 in savings and investments. If you feel you need $2,000 per month, then you should have saved $600,000. If you feel you need $3,000 per month, you should have saved $900,000, and so on.

The Value of Human Capital

There's a good chance some of you may just now be regaining consciousness from the shock of reading that number. The idea of needing almost a million dollars just to produce $3,000 per month of income may seem like quite a lot. I assure you that when you consider the variables of inflation, life expectancy and the inconsistencies of investment returns in the stock market, it's a good rule of thumb. We'll talk more about the strategy behind this and how to invest those dollars in a few moments.

What this rule of thumb does underscore however, is the value of our human capital. We are all born with certain gifts. We each have unique strengths, talents and abilities that we develop throughout our childhood and adolescence. When we reach high school and college age, we supplement those gifts with formal education. We learn how to apply those gifts, how to harness and focus them toward specific projects and tasks. Eventually we get jobs and gain experience as we apply our developed gifts to the workplace. As we continue to work we gain even more experience that further develops those gifts until we finally become experts in our chosen fields.

These gifts, from the moment we are born until the day we die, represent our human capital, which is both our greatest personal asset as well as our greatest financial asset. Using this 300:1 ratio, let's examine a couple of different scenarios to demonstrate the value of your human capital.

Let's assume that you are age 55, have a household income of $60,000 per year and want to retire at age 67, the age at which you are currently eligible for full Social Security retirement benefits.

In scenario 1, let's further assume that you have saved $300,000 for retirement, and are able to continue to save 15% of your salary, or $9,000 per year into a retirement savings program like an IRA or 401(k). As such, to maintain your current standard of living you would need to have a retirement income goal of $51,000 per year ($60,000 current salary minus $9,000 contribution to savings.) At age 67, based on current benefit schedules, you can expect approximately $23,000 per year in Social Security benefits, leaving approximately $28,000 per year to be generated from your own savings. Further assuming you can average a 7% return per year on your accumulated savings and investments as shown in Table 10.1, you can reasonably expect your investments to grow to the $900,000 or so needed to support an additional $3,000 per month of retirement income.

Age	Beginning Balance	Annual Contribution	Return	Ending Balance
55	$ 300,000	$9,000	7.00%	$ 330,630
56	$ 330,630	$9,000	7.00%	$ 363,404
57	$ 363,404	$9,000	7.00%	$ 398,472
58	$ 398,472	$9,000	7.00%	$ 435,995
59	$ 435,995	$9,000	7.00%	$ 476,145
60	$ 476,145	$9,000	7.00%	$ 519,105
61	$ 519,105	$9,000	7.00%	$ 565,072
62	$ 565,072	$9,000	7.00%	$ 614,257
63	$ 614,257	$9,000	7.00%	$ 666,885
64	$ 666,885	$9,000	7.00%	$ 723,197

65	$ 723,197	$9,000	7.00%	$ 783,451
66	$ 783,451	$9,000	7.00%	$ 847,923
67	$ 847,923	$9,000	7.00%	$ 916,907

Table 10.1 Scenario 1

The problem of course, is that our retirement income goal is a moving target. At 3.5% inflation it will now require approximately $77,000 per year at age 67 to maintain the same standard of living that $51,000 does at age 55. Now instead of making up a $28,000 per year annual shortfall, we need to make up closer $50,000 per year. (That is assuming that Social Security benefits remain payable at age 67 and increase with inflation as well.) Instead of reaching our goal with a little more than $900,000, it will now require more than $1.2 million!

The three choices we have here are pretty straightforward - either reduce your standard of living, delay retiring and continue working at your present job, or find another job with fewer hours and less pay to supplement your retirement income. For those who are dissatisfied with their current employment, staying for another 12 years until age 67 is a hard enough pill to swallow. The idea of staying beyond that becomes even more distasteful. But as many 60-somethings and older will tell us today, the reality of finding a new, even part-time job at age 67 in a new field in which you may or may not have appropriate experience and training can be very difficult, to say the least.

In our second scenario let's assume that we've adopted a pretirement mindset and changed our goal. Instead of proceeding with the goal of retiring at age 67, we are now more interested in finally doing whatever it is we've always wanted to do. That may mean not only additional education as we re-tool and re-train ourselves to acquire the skills necessary to go into our new field, but in many cases that also means a lower salary. In this case, let's assume a 25% reduction in salary to $45,000 per year. (Not that a lower salary is always the case. I had many clients who left one job only to continue to work as consultants or go into new fields that paid better than the career they just left.) Now, instead of working to retire away from a job at age 67, let's assume you enjoy what you're doing so much that you're willing, like my client Betty, to continue working it until at least age 75. With that being the case, you may choose to delay receiving Social Security benefits until age 70, at which time (according to current benefit schedules) you can expect to receive almost $29,000 per year. Even though your salary is lower, let's assume you still contribute 15%, and that you are still able to maintain a 7% return. Even though you are likely to trim expenses as a result of your new, potentially reduced salary, let's assume that we maintain the ultimate retirement income goal of $51,000 in today's dollars. Now, as Table 10.2 shows, you are able to grow your assets at age 75 to over $1.5 million.

Age	Beginning Balance	Annual Contribution	Return	Ending Balance
55	$ 300,000	$ 6,750	7.00%	$ 328,223
56	$ 328,223	$ 6,750	7.00%	$ 358,421
57	$ 358,421	$ 6,750	7.00%	$ 390,733
58	$ 390,733	$ 6,750	7.00%	$ 425,306
59	$ 425,306	$ 6,750	7.00%	$ 462,300
60	$ 462,300	$ 6,750	7.00%	$ 501,884
61	$ 501,884	$ 6,750	7.00%	$ 544,238
62	$ 544,238	$ 6,750	7.00%	$ 589,557
63	$ 589,557	$ 6,750	7.00%	$ 638,049
64	$ 638,049	$ 6,750	7.00%	$ 689,935
65	$ 689,935	$ 6,750	7.00%	$ 745,453
66	$ 745,453	$ 6,750	7.00%	$ 804,857
67	$ 804,857	$ 6,750	7.00%	$ 868,419
68	$ 868,419	$ 6,750	7.00%	$ 936,431
69	$ 936,431	$ 6,750	7.00%	$ 1,009,204
70	$ 1,009,204	$ 6,750	7.00%	$ 1,087,071
71	$ 1,087,071	$ 6,750	7.00%	$ 1,170,388
72	$ 1,170,388	$ 6,750	7.00%	$ 1,259,538
73	$ 1,259,538	$ 6,750	7.00%	$ 1,354,928
74	$ 1,354,928	$ 6,750	7.00%	$ 1,456,995
75	$ 1,456,995	$ 6,750	7.00%	$ 1,566,207

Table 10.2 Scenario 2

Now, using our 300:1 ratio and 4% withdrawal rate, you can now safely generate over $60,000 per year from your investments.

When combined with Social Security of $29,000, you are able to well exceed your inflated retirement income goal of $79,500.

Obviously I recognize that even in this case we're making a lot of assumptions. Will you be able to find a job that you truly enjoy that pays 75% of what you currently earn? Will you be able to keep that job until you're 75? Will your health hold out and allow you to work as long as you want to? The fact is there are a lot of unknowns that we simply don't have the answers to. But that's OK. What we're really talking about here is not so much financial security, but quality of life. If you love your job and can see yourself enjoying staying there until traditional retirement age and then transitioning into a traditional retirement - great! Be grateful for your good fortune as you are no doubt the envy of millions.

But if you are among the millions of walking wounded who can't wait to leave your job and are struggling to save enough for retirement, then holding out for retirement is a fool's goal. True financial independence as envisioned in most of our retirement dreams is becoming constantly more difficult to achieve. Do you really want to spend another 10 or 15 years or more doing something that's grown tired and dull in pursuit of a goal that is constantly moving further away from you anyway? Wouldn't it be better to focus on creating the life you want today, and then continue that life well beyond what is considered a normal retirement age?

If your left-brain is still looking for more proof, let me offer this. According to a *Retirement Savings and Household Wealth in 2007* report that was updated and released in April of 2009 by the Congressional Research Service, only 53% of U.S. households owned at least one retirement account of any kind in 2007, whether it was an IRA, a 401(k) plan or some other employment-based retirement account. Of that 53%, the median combined balance of all retirement accounts within the household was $45,000. Twenty-five percent of households had total retirement account balances of $140,000 or more, and 25% of households had total retirement account balances of $11,000 or less. Knowing this, let's take a look at a scenario that might be more applicable to a larger number of people.

In this third scenario, let's assume that the total of all retirement account assets is $100,000, which happens to be the median value of all retirement accounts owned by households headed by persons between the ages of 55 and 64 in 2007, according to this same Congressional Research Service report. Using the same set of assumptions that you are able to save 15% of your $60,000 per year income, have a retirement income goal now of $77,000 based on inflation of 3.5% and are able to generate a return of 7%, you see now in Table 10.3 that you will still fall significantly short of your goal.

Age	Beginning Balance	Annual Contribution	Return	Ending Balance
55	$ 100,000	$ 9,000	7.00%	$ 116,630
56	$ 116,630	$ 9,000	7.00%	$ 134,424
57	$ 134,424	$ 9,000	7.00%	$ 153,464
58	$ 153,464	$ 9,000	7.00%	$ 173,836
59	$ 173,836	$ 9,000	7.00%	$ 195,635
60	$ 195,635	$ 9,000	7.00%	$ 218,959
61	$ 218,959	$ 9,000	7.00%	$ 243,916
62	$ 243,916	$ 9,000	7.00%	$ 270,621
63	$ 270,621	$ 9,000	7.00%	$ 299,194
64	$ 299,194	$ 9,000	7.00%	$ 329,768
65	$ 329,768	$ 9,000	7.00%	$ 362,481
66	$ 362,481	$ 9,000	7.00%	$ 397,485
67	$ 397,485	$ 9,000	7.00%	$ 434,939

Table 10.3 Scenario 3

Using our 300:1 ratio, the $434,000 in accumulated assets will produce approximately $17,000 per year of income. Combined with the $23,000 we expect from Social Security, that leaves us well short of our retirement income goal of $77,000. For the majority of boomers and Generation Jones, the reality is that continued work beyond normal retirement age will indeed be required. As such, finding work you love, and doing it now so you can secure a position in that industry, may be the most important factor to achieving happiness in the second half of life.

The Impact of Controlling Expenses

To recognize the impact that controlling our expenses has on our financial freedom, we can use the same 300:1 rule of thumb. If you need $300,000 in investment assets to produce $1,000 of monthly income, that also means that for every $1,000 that you can reduce your monthly living expenses, you can also reduce your savings accumulation number by $300,000! Rather than working on accumulating more assets, let's focus on reducing our expenses.

For many of us, the idea of controlling our expenses has a negative connotation. We associate the idea of budgeting with denying ourselves of the things we want. The reality is that budgeting allows us to choose between the short-term meeting of a desire, and the long-term achievement of our priorities. As mentioned earlier, it is simple human nature to want more. But for most of us, our resources to obtain all the things we want are limited. By being mindful and attentive about how and where they spend their money, the Financially Mature are able to utilize their limited resources to achieve their most important goals. The Financially Mature gladly concede their short-term desires in favor of their longer-term goals.

The key to cutting your expenses then is to make sure the areas you cut are short-term desires, not long-term priorities. The first step in doing that is to ensure you have a clear vision of your priorities. In Chapters 5 and 6 we talked about creating balance among the Six Key Life Arenas and how to create a sense of purpose in your life. We also talked about identifying your priorities and creating a clear vision of what you want your life to be. If you haven't already done so, now would be a good time to go back and complete some of those exercises.

Assuming that you do have a clear vision of your priorities, the next step is to determine if your spending is aligned with those priorities. Many people are truly surprised to see how much of their money is actually spent on short-term comfort items that are not consistent with their long-term goals. By comparing your actual spending with your priorities you can uncover places to cut back that will not have a significant impact on your long-term goals or your short-term quality of life. The best way to do that is to begin tracking your expenses.

In our personal cash flow statement we categorized expenses as being either fixed or variable. Fixed expenses include the amounts that we save for our emergency fund, retirement, college education funding and other savings goals such as a new car fund, new house fund, or a transition fund if we want to start a new career. Other fixed expenses included any non-monthly, periodic expenses such as homeowner association dues or property taxes, recurring expenses such as utilities, and debt service to repay any amounts that you have borrowed. Variable expenses are also divided between those expenses that are necessary, such as food, and discretionary expenses such as dining out and various forms of entertainment.

While our divvying up of expenses in this manner is good for ensuring that we include all of our expenses for planning purposes, it's not how we initially think about it. When you look at a grocery receipt you don't think of it as a variable-necessity expense, you think of it as groceries. You consider the mortgage payment just that - a mortgage payment - not debt service. Even though each of these expenses will be categorized according to what we've laid out, for discussion purposes here we're going to talk in more everyday terms.

To reduce expenses, we need to look at how much of our total income each category of expense consumes. A typical family budget of after-tax, take-home pay might look something like Figure 10.4.

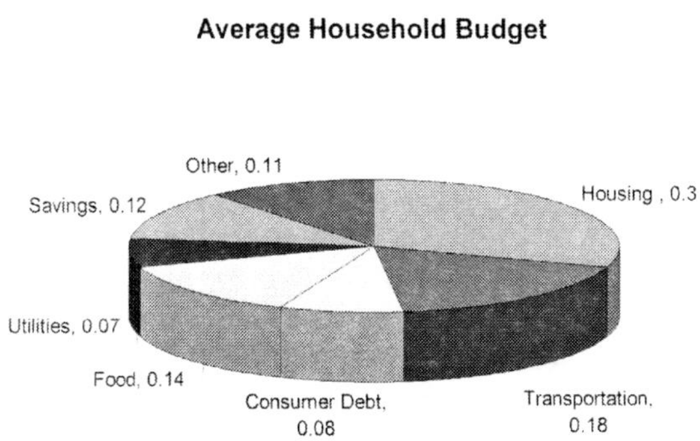

Figure 10.4
Typical Family Budget

To break this down even further take a look at Table 10.5.

		Percent of Monthly Income
Housing		
	Mortgage Payment	24%
	Property Taxes	3%
	HOA	1%
	Maintenance	2%
	Insurance	<1%
Transportation		
	Car Loan	10%
	Fuel	6%
	Service	1%
	Insurance	1%
Consumer Debt		
	Dept Store Card	2%
	Gen Credit Card	5%
	Gas Card	1%
Food		
	Groceries	9%
	Dining Out	5%
Utilities		
	Total	7%
Savings		
	Retirement	10%
	Education	1%
	Emergency Fund	1%
Everything Else		
	Entertainment	6%
	Household	3%
	Misc	2%
Total		100%

Table 10.5
Typical Family Budget Details

The first thing to notice in this "typical American family budget" is that over 40% of it is being spent on debt service! Between the mortgage (24%), car payments (10%) and credit cards

(8%) a total of 42% of the typical family budget goes toward paying off loans. When you add the additional 34% that goes toward periodic, recurring and the variable-necessity expenses of food, utilities, insurance, property taxes and more, a total of 76% of the typical American's income is going toward areas that support our standard of living but may not support our quality of life.

If we indeed define financial freedom as the ability to spend our time as we please without the obligations and responsibilities that create worry and stress around money, then we would want as little of our income as possible going to those things we feel we *have* to pay, but rather toward those things we want to pay - our discretionary expenses. The things we have to pay include our debt service, recurring and periodic fixed expenses as well as our variable-necessity expenses. The things we want to allocate our money toward include savings and variable-discretionary expenses. We want the freedom spend our time and money as we choose, not how we feel we have to spend it. The big house, fancy car and designer clothes all add to our standard of living, but do they really add to our quality of life? Do those things align with our long-term priorities or do they simply satisfy short-term desires?

The reality is that the two areas that create financial freedom are our savings expense and our variable-discretionary spending. The more of our income we can allocate to these two areas, the more financial freedom we'll enjoy. These are the budget areas that create confidence in your financial plan and freedom from stress and worry over money. By allocating at least 10% of your income to long-term saving and 1% to an emergency fund, you create a financial cushion that should your income be interrupted, you will still be able to maintain your lifestyle. That preparation, as a key element to becoming Financially Mature, provides a sense of confidence and peace of mind. Instead of worrying about the next paycheck, you can rest easy in the confidence of knowing that if the next paycheck is interrupted, either voluntarily because you chose to make changes or involuntarily due to circumstances beyond your control, you have the resources to maintain your quality of life.

Reducing Debt

As typically the largest single "have to pay" expense, reducing the amount you pay to service your debt can have the biggest impact on your feeling of financial freedom. Obviously the ideal situation is to completely eliminate all of your debt. Not only does that improve your balance sheet, but it also reduces the amount of income you're required to bring in each month.

"Now hold on," you might be thinking. "Isn't some debt, like a mortgage against my house that is tax-deductible, a good thing to have?" In my opinion, assuming your goal is achieve financial freedom, the answer is a flat-out "no".

The mortgage interest deduction is, in my opinion, one of the biggest financial misperceptions out there. Now in some cases, especially when you have significant other itemized deductions on your tax return, it can make sense. But those "ifs" are often overlooked in the equation. The assumption is that the mortgage interest deduction is good for everybody. The reality is that in a lot of cases the benefit isn't as great as we might think. Remember that the mortgage interest deduction is just that - a deduction - not a tax credit. A deduction means you are able to reduce your taxable income by the amount of interest you pay. Depending on your tax rate you'll likely owe between 15% - 35% of your taxable income, which means for every dollar you pay in interest, you only receive a tax break of that same 15-35%. That leaves 65% - 85% of every interest dollar still flowing away from you.

Remember also that the benefit of that deduction needs to be determined by comparing the total of all your itemized deductions against the standard deduction. For 2009-2010 the standard deduction for a married couple filing jointly is $11,400, which means the additional benefit of the mortgage interest deduction has to be measured by the amount above the standard deduction. If, for example, you have a $250,000 mortgage at 5.5% you will pay $13,750 in mortgage interest throughout the year. If you are in the 28% tax bracket and the mortgage interest was your only significant itemized deduction, then that mortgage will save you $3,850 in income taxes. ($13,750 x 28% = $3,850.) Compared to the standard deduction savings of $3,192 ($11,400 x 28%) that everyone is entitled to regardless of whether or not they have a mortgage, that means the real tax benefit of the $13,750 paid in interest may equate down to a mere $658 ($13,750 - $13,192.)

That is not to say that home ownership is not a good investment - it is. But from the perspective of achieving financial freedom, the tax benefits of carrying a huge mortgage do not outweigh the flexibility that can be achieved by eliminating your debt.

12 Steps to Pay Down Debt

So how do you go about systematically paying down your debt? I've found these 12 steps make all the difference in the world.

1. Make sure your cash flow is balanced or positive so you do not continue to accumulate debt. Usually the accumulation of debt is the result of unconscious overspending. By tracking your spending using a personal cash flow statement, you can see immediately where you are spending, and by how much you may be spending above your income. Balancing your cash flow often requires difficult lifestyle choices but is critical to achieving Financial Maturity and the financial freedom that goes along with it.

2. When your cash flow is balanced, make a list of all your debts including the creditor, the balance owed, the interest rate that you're paying on each debt, and the monthly payment amount for each debt. All of this information should be compiled for your personal balance sheet as well.

3. Total the monthly payment column to determine how much you're paying each month in total debt service.

4. Group your debts into short-term (those that can be paid off within 6 months), intermediate-term (those

that will be paid off between 7 and 60 months) and long-term (those that will take more than 60 months to pay.) Again, this same information can be used for your balance sheet.

5. If there are any debts with small balances that can be paid off in the next 3-4 months, keep those separate and work to pay those off as quickly as possible. This will help your credit score and loosen up cash flow that can be applied to other payments.

6. Explore consolidating any intermediate-term or long-term debts that carry high interest rates into one lower-interest loan. Your goals in doing this are to reduce your interest rates and the total amount of your monthly payments. However, be careful not to lower your payment purely by extending the length of time it will take to repay the loan.

7. When you have finished grouping and consolidating your debt, you should be able to categorize each debt as short-term, intermediate-term or long-term, and all should have reasonable interest rates.

8. Focus first on paying off your smaller balances. When you completely pay one off, take the payment amount that you had been paying and add that to the next smallest balance. By paying that much extra each month, you will pay the next loan off that much quicker. Continue to "snowball" your payments like this until all of your short-term debts are completely paid.

9. Take half the amount you were paying on your short-term debts and begin contributing that to an emergency fund savings account. Many people ask if it is better to begin to save or to pay down debt. The fact is we want to do both. But if your cash flow is negative, you need to concentrate on paying down debt. As soon

as your cash flow turns positive however, let's take part of that and begin to build up savings.

10. Take the other half of what you were paying to service your short-term debt, and add that amount to the monthly payment of your smallest-balance, intermediate-term debt. When one is paid off, continue to "snowball" these payments by applying the amount of the now-paid debt to your next lowest balance payment. Continue this process until all intermediate-term debts are paid.

11. Again, take half the amount you were paying toward your intermediate-term debts and begin to contribute that toward savings and investments.

12. Apply the other half of your intermediate-term payment toward paying down your long-term debt in the same fashion as before.

By continuing to watch your spending and focus on paying down your debt, you will eventually become completely debt-free.

Cutting Other Expenses

Determining where else you can cut back to reduce your monthly spending is a highly personal choice. Some, like my clients Tom and Sue whose children thought bringing Coke into the house was a treat, are masters at living very frugally and seemed to not only not miss the little comforts and conveniences, they actually took pleasure in seeing just how inexpensively they could live. I will admit, I myself could probably not live that way. But that's OK as long as I'm aware of the choices I make.

The problem is that many of us are not aware of the "leaks" in our monthly cash flow that consume a significant portion of our money but add very little to our quality of life. The $4 cup of coffee (which I'll admit I love) if indulged on five days a week could easily cost me over $1,000 a year! Said another way, using our 300:1 ratio, I would need to accumulate over $25,000 in investment assets to sustain that $4 per day coffee habit. When looked at that way, I don't mind brewing my own at home.

That, I believe, is really what's important about this topic. It's not about denying yourself the things you love or the little comforts and luxuries you might have grown accustomed to. It's about setting your priorities and making conscious decisions based on those priorities.

If you need help gathering ideas about where you can cut your expenses, there are some great tips available at a number of very good web sites.

nfcc.org - This web site from the National Foundation for Credit Counseling provides some great tips on financial education and budgeting.

betterbudgeting.com - This site provides hundreds of practical tips and hints about everything from using coupons to how to save money on vacations.

fpaforfinancialplanning.org - This is the consumer education site of the Financial Planning Association. It provides a number of resources for budgeting and various other life goals.

Chapter 11

Create an Investment Process

Deciding where to put your money or how to construct the investment asset portion of your balance sheet can be a difficult task. Not only is there a ton of information out there, but it seems like everybody - from your father-in-law to your neighbor to your beer drinking buddies to the financial advisor you met at your book club - all have opinions about what you should do. The problem is that there is so much misinformation out there that those who think they know what they are doing often end up giving some of the worst advice possible. I remember one client who was a perfect example.

Jennifer was a mid-level human resources manager in her late 30s who called me one day and asked me to sell a sizeable chunk of an investment that had been set aside for her 7-year-old daughter's college education. She told me that a friend of hers had invested in a small company whose stock was trading around $6.00 per share. "My friend got in when the thing was less than a buck a share. She's made over six times her money in just three months! They say it's going all the way to $60 a share!"

While I tried to warn Jennifer of the risks, you can probably guess what happened next. Sure enough by the time Jennifer got in the stock was trading at over $8.00 per share and within two weeks plummeted back down to less than a buck. She essentially lost seven years worth of savings by taking advice from someone who was in no position to give it.

That I believe, is lesson Number 1. There is no shortage of people out there who are more than willing to tell you what you should do with your money. The problem is that very few of them are qualified to do so. There is often such a distrust of financial advisors that people are willing to listen to anybody. Often times we tend to think that if someone is a successful doctor, lawyer or business executive, they must know what to do with their money also, right? Unfortunately that is very wrong. Some of the most successful professionals are very good at what they do, but have no idea how to invest their money. They are different skills and different knowledge bases. Even if they do know how to invest their own money, they probably have no idea how to invest yours. The idea that "if it works for you, it must also work for me" is a very dangerous assumption when it comes to investing. Your goals, risk tolerance and timeframes may all be very different. Therefore, what is appropriate for one person is not necessarily appropriate for another. In the last chapter, we'll talk about different types of financial advisors and how to select a good one, but the bottom line is that you need to be very careful about whom you select to provide investment advice.

With that said, why should you listen to me? Because I'm not going to tell you where to invest your money, I'm going to give you a process so you can determine for yourself the best way to invest your money.

Step 1
Define Your Buckets

The first step in determining how to invest your money is to separate your investments into buckets based on your goals and timeframes. For example, when I left my last employer, I knew I was going to be unemployed for some time and also that it would take a while to re-establish an income stream. Based on that, I looked at my goals and priorities.

Goal/priority #1 - Take care of my family while I found appropriate work. How long did I think I was going to be unemployed and how much would we need to get through that stretch? By looking at our monthly expenses and cutting back in areas that would not affect our lifestyle, my wife and I came up with a number that we felt we could live on each month. We then estimated how long it would take to re-establish an income stream up to that amount. Based on those two figures we were able to come up with an amount needed for our "transition fund" that would support the family after I left my job. By saving a portion of my income for several months before leaving and reallocating some other savings that we had, we were able to create this transition fund before I left that last employer. Obviously this was an immediate, short-term goal.

Goal/priority #2 - New business start-up. For me, the idea that I had for my new business was going to require some additional training and some start-up business capital. Fortunately these costs were relatively small, but we did have to make some tough decisions regarding other goals that we had allocated that money toward. This too was a short-term goal.

Goal/priority #3 – Retirement. Even though my goal was to "pretire" - to find purposeful work that I could balance with all the other priorities in my life and continue for many, many years - I still, as many of us do, hope to make working for pay optional some day. As such, I wanted to continue to allow my retirement accounts to grow, as retirement remains a long-term goal.

Goal/priority #4 - Provide for my children's college education. This is a highly personal choice. When I talked with my clients about funding their children's college education, I would always ask, "How much of their education do you feel is your responsibility to provide?" Some parents feel that if the child wants to go to Harvard or become a doctor, it's their parental responsibility to get them there. Others feel that filling the car up with gas so their child can get to the campus is as far as their responsibility goes. There is no right answer. But based on what my wife and I felt was our responsibility, we wanted to continue to fund that goal. With children in elementary and junior high school, this was an intermediate-term goal.

You may have other goals, but as you can see the process of identifying them and separating them into buckets is fairly straightforward. For each goal, figure out how much money you're going to need and the monthly funding required to accumulate that amount. Whether you're starting with a small amount and will continue adding to it each month, or if you have already accumulated what you'll need for that goal, proceed on to step 2.

Step 2
Determine a Broad Asset Allocation for Each Bucket

The second step of our investment process is to determine an asset allocation for each bucket. Asset allocation is simply an investment term for doing what your mother always told you - don't put all your eggs in one basket. By diversifying your investments into different asset classes, you can reduce the volatility and risk of any one class. As we discussed in Chapter 9, different kinds of investments have different risk and reward characteristics. Cash equivalents like savings accounts and CDs are considered very low risk, but also generate a very low return. Stocks and stock mutual funds have the potential for higher returns, but can also lose a portion (or even all) of your principal. Asset allocation is simply a term for describing how much (what percentage) of your assets you are going to allocate (diversify) to these different types of investments.

Defining a specific asset allocation is typically a two-stage process that involves three factors - the timeframe involved, the investor's risk tolerance, and the asset categories to be included. In the first stage we define a broad allocation among the three basic asset classes - stocks, bonds and cash equivalents. In the second stage we look at sub-asset class allocations. Sub-asset class allocations look specifically at what types of stocks or bonds we might include. Our stock allocation, for example, might be divided up further to specifically determine the percentage of growth stocks or value stocks we might include, or how many U.S. versus foreign company stocks. On the bond side, we might look at the percentage of short-term or long-term bonds, or the percentages between U.S. government bonds, corporate bonds or foreign government bonds. Additional asset classes like real estate, gold or commodities might also be included in this second stage. We'll talk more about this second stage in step 3.

The first stage of our asset allocation process, however, is to look at our allocation in very broad terms based primarily on the timeframe of the investment. The fact is, if you are going to need the money in the next two to three years, that very fact dictates that the allocation should be nearly 100% cash equivalents. The timeframe for that goal is so short that if you were to invest in any variable-rate investment and it went down in value, there is just no time to wait for it to come back. Further, since cash equivalents are the only risk-free place to put money, there's no reason to consider other asset classes. A short-term asset allocation would likely be 100% cash equivalents such as savings accounts and CDs as shown in Figure 11.1.

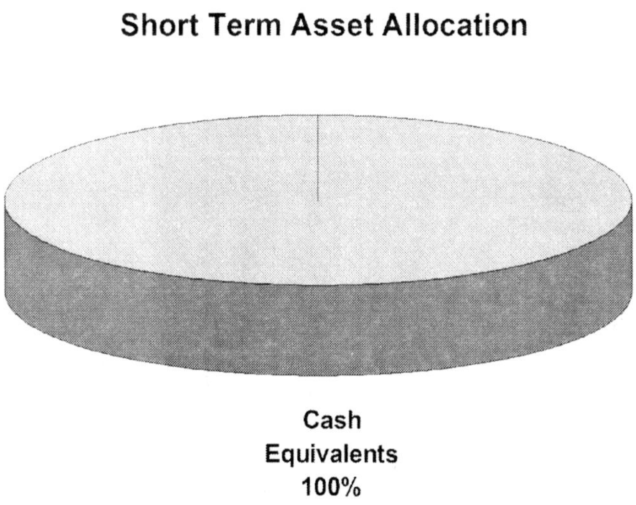

Figure 11.1

As the timeframes increase, you can afford to take more risk. For an intermediate-term goal of say four to seven years, you might consider an allocation as illustrated in Figure 11.2 made up primarily of bonds (say 50%) but possibly including small percentages of stocks (20%) and cash equivalents (30%). As your timeframes increase, your risk tolerance becomes more of a factor. Do you have other resources you could draw from if this investment were to go down during that timeframe? Is your timeframe flexible so that you could wait a couple of extra years? How comfortable are you with the ups and downs of the market?

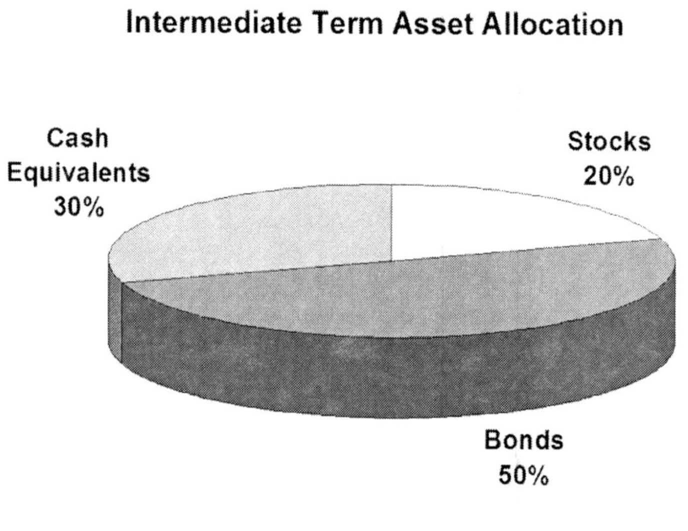

Figure 11.2

As your timeframes begin to stretch out to ten years or more, your risk tolerance becomes the most important factor. The conventional wisdom is that the longer timeframe you have, the more risk you can and should take. But regardless of your timeframe, if your investments are causing you stress and worry from the ups and downs of the market, you are definitely investing too aggressively. (Remember - financial freedom is being free from the stress and worry that money causes in our lives. That doesn't just refer to not having enough of it, it also refers to how we manage and invest it.)

That doesn't mean however, that we should avoid risk altogether. Loss of purchasing power through inflation is another significant risk to your long-term financial well-being. At 3.5% annual inflation, it will take twice as much money - $100,000 - in 20 years to purchase the same goods and services that $50,000 can purchase today.

Historically, stock investments have proven to be the best hedge against long-term inflation, but they come with risk and volatility. Just how much risk and volatility you can live with is different for each of us. Not only is our risk tolerance influenced by our logical reasoning and knowledge of investments, but also by our emotions of greed and fear. As we sit in the comfortable confines of our financial advisor's office or at home in front of a computer and logically examine the historical returns and volatility of different investments, we can easily come up with an asset allocation that makes perfect rational sense. But as we've discussed, when the markets start to move, that rational reasoning often goes out the window as our emotions take over. Just how much movement you can accept before your emotions take over is your risk tolerance. For this part, we have to get a bit more technical.

One way to look at how much movement a particular portfolio might experience is to look at its standard deviation. Standard deviation is just a fancy term for normal movement of a stock price. The standard deviation measures the normal price swings that an investment experiences around its average mean return. The best way to understand this is to look at the historical returns of the three primary asset classes in Table 11.3.

Annual Returns 1928 -2008								
Year	Stocks	T-Bills	T-Notes		Year	Stocks	T-Bills	T-Notes
1928	43.81%	3.08%	0.84%		1970	3.56%	6.69%	16.75%
1929	-8.30%	3.16%	4.20%		1971	14.22%	4.54%	9.79%
1930	-25.12%	4.55%	4.54%		1972	18.76%	3.95%	2.82%
1931	-43.84%	2.31%	-2.56%		1973	-14.31%	6.73%	3.66%
1932	-8.64%	1.07%	8.79%		1974	-25.90%	7.78%	1.99%
1933	49.98%	0.96%	1.86%		1975	37.00%	5.99%	3.61%
1934	-1.19%	0.32%	7.96%		1976	23.83%	4.97%	15.98%
1935	46.74%	0.18%	4.47%		1977	-6.98%	5.13%	1.29%
1936	31.94%	0.17%	5.02%		1978	6.51%	6.93%	-0.78%
1937	-35.34%	0.30%	1.38%		1979	18.52%	9.94%	0.67%
1938	29.28%	0.08%	4.21%		1980	31.74%	11.22%	-2.99%
1939	-1.10%	0.04%	4.41%		1981	-4.70%	14.30%	8.20%
1940	-10.67%	0.03%	5.40%		1982	20.42%	11.01%	32.81%
1941	-12.77%	0.08%	-2.02%		1983	22.34%	8.45%	3.20%
1942	19.17%	0.34%	2.29%		1984	6.15%	9.61%	13.73%
1943	25.06%	0.38%	2.49%		1985	31.24%	7.49%	25.71%
1944	19.03%	0.38%	2.58%		1986	18.49%	6.04%	24.28%
1945	35.82%	0.38%	3.80%		1987	5.81%	5.72%	-4.96%
1946	-8.43%	0.38%	3.13%		1988	16.54%	6.45%	8.22%
1947	5.20%	0.57%	0.92%		1989	31.48%	8.11%	17.69%
1948	5.70%	1.02%	1.95%		1990	-3.06%	7.55%	6.24%
1949	18.30%	1.10%	4.66%		1991	30.23%	5.61%	15.00%
1950	30.81%	1.17%	0.43%		1992	7.49%	3.41%	9.36%
1951	23.68%	1.48%	-0.30%		1993	9.97%	2.98%	14.21%
1952	18.15%	1.67%	2.27%		1994	1.33%	3.99%	-8.04%
1953	-1.21%	1.89%	4.14%		1995	37.20%	5.52%	23.48%
1954	52.56%	0.96%	3.29%		1996	23.82%	5.02%	1.43%
1955	32.60%	1.66%	-1.34%		1997	31.86%	5.05%	9.94%
1956	7.44%	2.56%	-2.26%		1998	28.34%	4.73%	14.92%
1957	-10.46%	3.23%	6.80%		1999	20.89%	4.51%	-8.25%
1958	43.72%	1.78%	-2.10%		2000	-9.03%	5.76%	16.66%
1959	12.06%	3.26%	-2.65%		2001	-11.85%	3.67%	5.57%
1960	0.34%	3.05%	11.64%		2002	-21.97%	1.66%	15.12%
1961	26.64%	2.27%	2.06%		2003	28.36%	1.03%	0.38%
1962	-8.81%	2.78%	5.69%		2004	10.74%	1.23%	4.49%
1963	22.61%	3.11%	1.68%		2005	4.83%	3.01%	2.87%
1964	16.42%	3.51%	3.73%		2006	15.61%	4.68%	1.96%
1965	12.40%	3.90%	0.72%		2007	5.48%	4.64%	10.21%
1966	-9.97%	4.84%	2.91%		2008	-36.58%	1.59%	20.10%
1967	23.80%	4.33%	-1.58%					
1968	10.81%	5.26%	3.27%		Average	11.09%	3.79%	5.44%
1969	-8.24%	6.56%	-5.01%					

Table 11.3
Annual Returns of
Three Primary Asset Classes

Shaded in each column are the best and worst years for each asset class since 1928. At the end of the chart is the average return for each asset class from 1928 through 2008. For stocks, you can see the best year was in 1954 when the market rose 52.56%, and the worst year was in 1931 when stocks were down 43.84%. While the average return was a very respectable 11.09%, investors had to suffer through a range of returns that covered almost 100 percentage points! 10-year Treasury notes averaged 5.44% but ranged from a negative 8.25% in 1999 to a positive 32.81% in 1982. T-bills, while providing a modest average return of 3.79% on the other hand, fluctuated very little from a single year best of over 14% in 1981 to a low of only .03% in 1940. Obviously 1940 was not much of a return, but at least it was still positive!

If you look at the average returns of each asset class, you'll notice that not once in any given year did any of these asset classes ever return an amount equal to their average. They always return either higher or lower than the average. Standard deviation is a measurement that tells you how much higher or lower than the average you can expect your returns to be, and how often that will occur.

Now I won't go into the mathematical formula to attempt to show how to calculate the standard deviation of any given investment, but there are a few things about it that are important to know. First of all, standard deviation is a statistical measure indicating both the range of returns around the average, and how often those returns are expected to fall within that range. For example, let's say we have an investment with an average return of 10% and a standard deviation of 20%. What that is telling us is that approximately two-thirds (67%) of the time, the return on that investment will be within one standard deviation measure of the average. That means that two out of every three years we can expect the return on that investment to be somewhere between *negative* 10% and positive 30%. (Take the average return of 10% plus or minus the standard deviation of 20% and you get a range between -10 and +30.) 95% of the time, or 95 years out of 100, we would expect the return to fall within two standard deviation measures of the average. In this example that would mean that 95% of the time we would expect a return between negative 30 and positive 50. (Again, take the average return of 10% and add/subtract two times the standard deviation{2 x 20 =40} and you get a range of -30 to +50.) Obviously the lower the standard deviation number, the less volatile the investment is.

When you take the returns of our three asset classes in Table 11.3 and plot them out on a graph as in Figure 11.4, the effects of standard deviation become easily apparent to see. T-bills, while averaging only 3.79% returned between a positive 3% and a positive 5% 22 times out of the 81 years we looked at in the Table. Further, the returns were between 0% and 7% seventy-one times. With a very narrow historical standard deviation of approximately 2%, you won't get many surprises with T- bills.

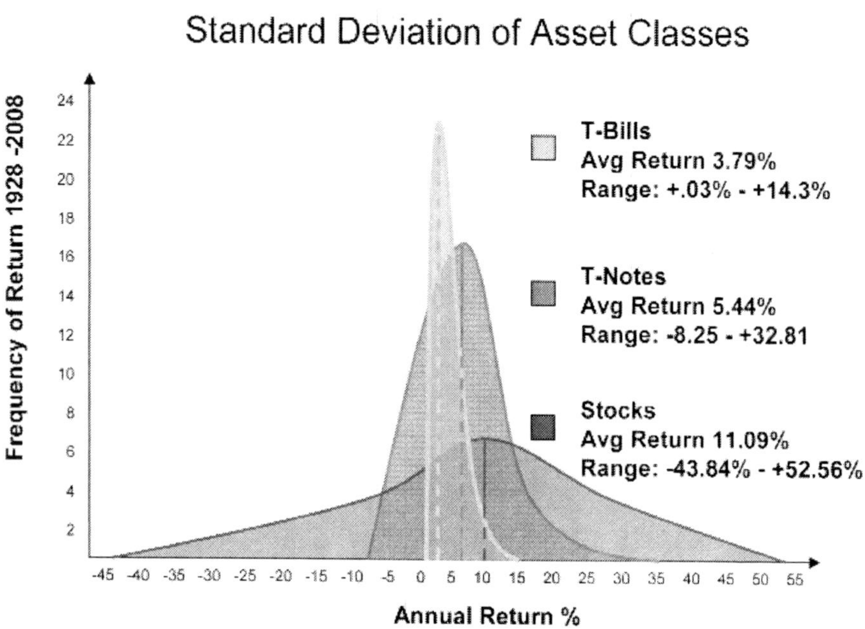

Figure 11.4
The Standard Deviation of Various Asset Classes

Stocks on the other hand, as you can see, have a huge standard deviation, historically averaging around 20%. That means that returns like 2008's -36%, while unusual, is not at all completely unexpected. That's where your risk tolerance needs to come into play. By diversifying our investments into different asset classes, you can reduce some of this volatility, but not all of it. Figuring out how much loss you are willing to bear will dictate what percentage of your assets need to be in safer, less volatile investments, and how much should be in more aggressive investments. For this reason, your risk tolerance becomes a large factor in determining an appropriate asset allocation. Examples of a conservative, moderate or aggressive long-term asset allocation are shown in Figures 11.5, 11.6 and 11.7 below. Yours can be anywhere in between (or beyond) these examples.

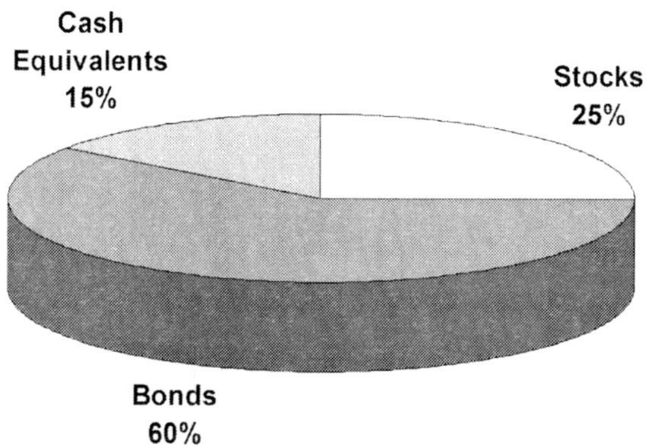

Figure 11.5
A Conservative Long-term Asset Allocation

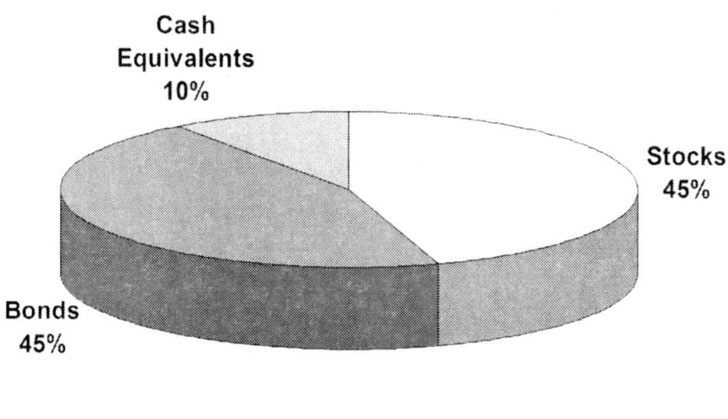

Figure 11.6
A Moderate Long-term Asset Allocation

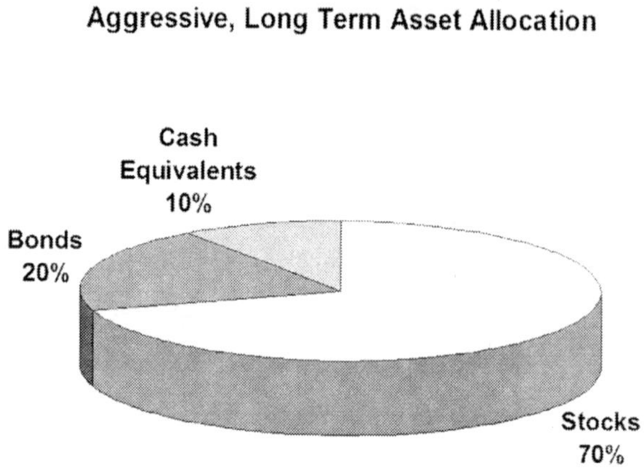

Figure 11.7
An Aggressive Long-term Asset Allocation

Step 3
Define Your Investment Philosophy

The third step in the investment decision process is to decide on an investment management philosophy - how do you want your money managed? When it comes to this decision, there are two broad choices - Strategic Asset Management or Tactical Asset Management.

Strategic Asset Management

The more widely accepted investment philosophy, especially among financial advisors, is known as Strategic Asset Management. Also commonly referred to as a "buy and hold" approach, strategic asset management utilizes a more detailed asset allocation plan. It uses various sub-asset categories to determine an optimal portfolio based on the targeted returns and the amount of risk the investor is willing to accept. This strategy is sometimes referred to as a "static" investment philosophy because once the asset allocation is set, it typically remains unchanged except as triggered by life events of the investor.

For example, let's say we were to adopt a strategic asset management philosophy and started with a moderate asset allocation of 10% cash equivalents, 45% stock and 45% bonds like we just mentioned. This portfolio might be broken down further into various sub-asset categories as follows:

Stocks:		
	Large Cap* Growth	10%
	Small Cap Growth	5%
	Large Cap Value	10%
	Mid Cap Value	5%
	Foreign Large Cap	10%
	Emerging Markets	5%
Bonds:		
	Intermediate-Term Treasuries	15%
	Intermediate-Term Corporate	15%
	Foreign	10%
	Gold**	5%
Cash Equivalents:		
	Savings accounts	5%
	T-bills	5%

*The term "Cap" refers to the market capitalization of the company - i.e. the price per share multiplied by the number of shares outstanding. In terms of asset allocation, the distinction is used to differentiate between large, medium and small companies. Large cap simply refers to those companies whose total outstanding stock is valued at over $5 billion dollars. Mid-cap stocks are typically those with a market capitalization between $1 and $5 billion, and small caps are those that have market capitalization of less than $1 billion.

**Gold is obviously not a bond, but as an asset allocation becomes more detailed, other asset classes like gold, commodities or real estate may be added. The amounts allocated to those classes need to come from somewhere, so in this case we are taking a percentage from the bond portion of the portfolio just to complete the example.

Once an asset allocation is determined, the strategic investor will stick with this asset allocation regardless of various fluctuations in the stock market or economy. The only moves that will be made will be to "rebalance" the portfolio. If for example, the stock portion of our sample portfolio performs very well such that those accounts now represent 55% of the portfolio, 10% of those stocks would be sold and reallocated to bonds or cash equivalents so that the portfolio is "rebalanced" back to its original 10/45/45 allocations.

The strategic philosophy is based on the rational evaluation and study of the various asset categories and their historical risk and return performance over time. The belief is that each asset class will continue to perform in the future somewhat similarly to what it has done in the past. Therefore if an investment such as T-bills has historically returned 3.79% with a 2% standard deviation, then we should expect it to continue to perform that way in the future. Similarly, if stocks average 10% (for example) but have a standard deviation of 20% (again, for example), then a negative return in stocks shouldn't be much of a surprise or concern to someone who has adopted a strategic philosophy. When those negative returns materialize, the strategic investor views them as inevitable but acceptable based on their long-term returns.

Given that belief, investors who adopt this strategy must adopt a long-term view of their investments, which at times can be quite difficult. As mentioned, this strategy is far more common among financial advisors because it doesn't require the advisor to attempt to "time" the market. (We'll talk more about that when we discuss tactical asset allocation.) The problem is that as we've discussed, the markets are not always rational. When fear and panic set in, the strategic investor is told to ride out the storm, that market volatility is inevitable and that in the end cooler heads will prevail. While this may in fact be true, the damage that can be done to an individual's portfolio while waiting for those cooler heads can sometimes be catastrophic. I'm reminded of the parade scene sequence from the movie *Animal House*. While chaos is erupting all around him, a young Kevin Bacon plays a college ROTC cadet who is coolly trying to tell everyone to "Remain calm. All is well." He then promptly gets trampled in the panic.

Another significant problem with strategic asset management has been identified by our friends in behavioral finance. As investors we tend to rely too heavily on our most recent experiences. As a result, our asset allocations get out of whack based on recent events. In the late 1990s when internet and growth stocks were surging, everybody wanted a piece of the action. We hadn't seen a serious decline in over 10 years (since Black Monday in 1987) and investors had grown used to steady gains of more than 20%. With nothing but the upside in our recent memories, investors began to look at asset allocation as 100% stocks and viewed diversification as spreading their money out among the various sub-asset categories of stocks alone. As we saw in 2000 however, when the stock markets started to fall and the irrational fears took over investor behavior, there was no difference between stock sub-asset categories. For the most part, they all went down. That short-term memory works against us in the opposite direction as well. After the market decline of 2008-2009, many investors became too conservative with their asset allocations and subsequently missed the large rally that materialized in the last three quarters of 2009.

The solution for someone who adopts a strategic asset management philosophy then is to set a realistic asset allocation that truly reflects the amount of risk (decline) they are willing to accept. An allocation with too much risk may lead to irrational, emotional decisions, while one with not enough risk may not allow you to reach your goals. Many firms and web sites provide risk-tolerance questionnaire's to help you determine your risk tolerance. One that I particularly like can be found at http://moneycentral.msn.com/investor/calcs/n_riskq/main.asp. This questionnaire examines both your capacity for risk as well as your risk tolerance.

Tactical Asset Management

The second choice in selecting an investment management philosophy is known as tactical asset management. Taken to its extreme, tactical asset management is also referred to as market timing - or attempting to predict when the markets will rise or fall and trade on those predictions. In that sense, tactical asset management is considered to be a purely speculative approach.

But those who have adopted a tactical asset management philosophy suggest that there are indeed known indicators that are useful in predicting the direction of not only the overall markets, but of individual stocks and sectors as well. They use a variety of techniques collectively known as technical analysis to look for patterns in a stock's price based largely on the irrational behavior of investors. When those patterns repeat themselves, the technical analyst is able to predict (based on past patterns) what the next move will be, and will trade on those anticipated moves. As such, the tactical investor is very active and will move money frequently in an attempt to maximize returns.

In my experience, the effectiveness of tactical asset management is a matter of degrees - just how far you can take it before it becomes speculation. On the one extreme, some tactical investors are truly day-traders, investing in and out of the markets on a daily basis based not at all on the fundamental quality of the company or its future prospects, but rather on the emotional sentiment of the day. Are people feeling good about this stock today? Has there been any news that might impact the company positively or negatively? What do the charts look like? Has there been momentum building in the stock? The number of minute details that can be analyzed and estimated are endless. Everything from "wave patterns" to volume indicators are used to predict where the stock price is headed.

The problem with this is that no one ever really knows what the future holds. Even if you assume that some patterns are reliable, those same patterns may become unreliable as more and more people attempt to use and trade off of that particular pattern. Even if you happen to predict one move correctly, it is virtually impossible to consistently, accurately predict what the markets are going to do. For that reason, most financial advisors stay away from a purely tactical approach.

Taken to a lesser degree, however, tactical asset management can be very useful in managing a basic asset allocation. For example, when we talked about how bonds work in Chapter 9, we indicated that there is an inverse but direct relationship between bond prices and interest rates. As interest rates go up, bond prices go down. An indirect but also generally accepted relationship is that when interest rates go up, stock prices also go down because fixed-interest bearing investments like cash equivalents and bonds become more attractive relative to stocks. As more money goes toward these new, higher-interest-paying bonds and cash equivalents, less money is available for stocks, which then go down in value based purely on decreased demand. The same is true in the opposite direction, as interest rates go down, the prices of existing bonds and stocks go up as they become better investments relative to new bonds being offered.

As such, a more moderate tactical investor will adjust their asset allocation based on these known relationships. When interest rates are near zero, the tactical investor knows that interest rates can't go below zero and therefore, eventually, there is only one way for them to go - up. As a result, the tactical investor will shorten their bond maturities or move their money to cash equivalents in anticipation of rising interest rates and the resulting decline in bond (and potentially in stock) prices. In times of economic recession the tactical investor will get rid of stocks of companies that are in highly cyclical industries such as automotive and leisure, and will invest in stocks of companies whose business is less affected by an economic downturn, such as food and energy companies.

In fact, this more moderate approach to tactical asset management is considered by many to be a hybrid between the strategic and tactical philosophies. A broad asset allocation is selected for each goal's bucket of money, and then actively managed and reallocated based on widely accepted, well-defined market indicators.

Step 4
Select Your Investment Vehicles

At this point you've divvyed money up into different buckets based on your goals, decided on a broad asset allocation for each bucket, and determined which investment philosophy you feel most comfortable with. Now you need to figure out which investment vehicles you are going to use to implement your strategy. For many people, this decision comes down to two questions: Do I believe active asset management adds value? And am I willing to pay for it?

Active asset management describes the value proposition of most mutual fund money managers. By using either fundamental or technical analysis, these managers evaluate the universe of stocks and bonds available to them and make selections based on which investments they feel will perform best and meet the objectives of the fund or account. As compared to you or me, these managers have access to far more information, (yes, even in the internet age). More importantly, they have the knowledge and ability to interpret that information to determine its relevance far better than most of us. But does having that information and the ability to decipher it result in better investment decisions? Unfortunately the evidence doesn't suggest so.

According to Standard & Poor's, which produces the *Indices versus Active Funds Scorecard*, in 2008 only about 25% of actively managed mutual funds beat their corresponding benchmark index. This means that if you just invested in everything that makes up the index without worrying about which ones might do well or poorly, you would have beaten 75% of the active-management professionals out there. (That assumes of course that you could actually invest in the index with no trading fees, commissions or account fees, which of course you can't.) One of the primary reasons for this is that fund managers, like any of us, charge for their services. The typical fund manager charges between 1-2% of assets annually for their services. That means they have to beat the index by at least that much just to match an unmanaged benchmark. For the 25% who are able to beat their comparable index, the rewards are obviously worth it.

So what are your choices? Here are the four most common investment vehicles you can use to implement your investment strategy.

Actively managed mutual funds

For the 25% of funds that beat their index, the rewards are well worth the costs. The problem here is in finding funds that consistently beat the index. Studies by Morningstar have shown that funds that perform at the top of their category in one year are in no better position than any other to continue that top ranking performance in subsequent years. While some funds and managers do consistently beat their peers and their related index, it's important to recognize that consistent outperformance is very difficult for even the best managers.

Passively managed mutual funds

Also known as index funds, these mutual funds don't attempt to add value by screening and selecting stocks that the managers feel will do better than others, but instead simply attempt to mirror whatever index they target. If the goal is to mirror the S&P 500 index, an index fund will hold the same 500 stocks in the same proportion as the index. Since there is no active management, research and very little trading of stocks, the fund management expenses for an index fund are typically less than .25% as compared to the 1-2% for most actively managed funds. The downside of course is that there is no potential to outperform the index nor is there hope for a manager to actively move you out of the market should the market begin to fall. With a passively managed index fund, you're in for the ride no matter what direction it goes.

Exchange Traded Funds (ETFs)

ETFs are similar to passively managed index funds and can play a role in either a strategic or tactical asset management strategy.

Because ETFs are essentially a basket of unmanaged stocks, their internal expenses are very low, making them a good choice for the long-term, buy-and-hold investor. At the same time, because they are able to be traded throughout the day, ETFs are typically a better alternative than funds when using an active tactical asset management strategy.

Separately Managed Accounts

Separately managed accounts are nothing more than brokerage accounts within which your money manager purchases stocks or other securities specifically for your account. Unlike actively managed mutual funds, index funds or ETFs where you purchase shares of a bundle of stocks, separately managed accounts allow you and your money manager to select individual investments specific to your needs. For example, let's say that you wanted to invest in large company stocks similar to the S&P 500, but did not want to invest in companies that produce tobacco products, have a poor record in how they treat their employees, or are involved in research you find objectionable. With a mutual fund or ETF you cannot specifically carve out those kinds of companies. With a separately managed account, you can define those limitations to exclude those kinds of investments from your account. With the rising popularity of the "green movement," more and more investors are becoming socially conscious about how their money is invested. And not just surrounding environmental concerns. They want to ensure that their money is being used to support the causes they care about, and not support companies or activities that are inconsistent with their values and beliefs.

Not surprisingly with this degree of customization, separately managed accounts are often the most expensive of the four alternatives, but they also give you the greatest choice and control over where your money is going.

Step 5
Decide if You Want to Work with an Advisor or Go It Alone

As you can see, the process for creating an investment portfolio that's aligned with your goals and personal investment philosophy is not necessarily an easy one. For those who have the time, discipline and interest to educate themselves, go through the asset allocation exercises and research various investments options it is certainly something that can be done on your own. In fact, many financial Eagles prefer to manage their investments on their own as it allows them to retain complete control. With the abundance of information available online, I believe this is a legitimate option for those who will take the time to stay up with what is happening. But if you don't have the time, discipline or interest to dedicate to managing your investments, you may want to work with a financial advisor.

That said however, it is still important to go through this process for two reasons. First, in the cases of steps 1 and 2, an advisor will ask about your goals, priorities and risk tolerance. The more well-thought-out guidance you can give your advisor the better chance your advisor has of coming up with a plan and an asset allocation that truly matches your needs. Second, by understanding the different investment approaches and implementation vehicles, you can select an advisor who manages money in a way that matches your expectations and philosophy. If you don't like the "buy-and-hold" approach of pure strategic management, you may have to search a bit more for an advisor who takes a hybrid or tactical approach. If you don't believe the value of active fund management is worth the cost, then you need to find an advisor who will work with index funds, ETFs and separately managed accounts.

I believe one of the primary reasons investors tend to be dissatisfied with their financial advisors is because of mismatched expectations. An investor may want or expect the advisor to move their money in a declining market. But if the advisor has adopted a long-term buy-and-hold approach, that's not going to happen. If you are going to work with an advisor, you need to take the time to find one who shares your philosophy. In the next chapter, I'll talk about the various ways that financial advisors get paid and how to select an advisor.

By going through the step-by-step process outlined above, you are much more likely to gain confidence knowing that you are managing and investing your money consistently with your overall life goals. Add to that the ability to manage and control your expenses, and you'll be well on your way to true financial freedom.

Converting Assets to Income

Once you have your money divided up into the various buckets, the question becomes: "How do you begin to withdraw money from those accounts to support your new lifestyle?" As you're beginning to see with so much of financial planning, there are several options available.

Interest Only Distributions

The first and simplest option is to take just the interest only out of your account. If you have a portfolio of $500,000 and are able to earn 5%, that would produce an annual income of $25,000. While many people tend to view this as a "safe" option because the plan is to not touch their principal, in fact this is an almost certain losing proposition.

There are two problems with an interest-only distribution option. The first is that interest rates change. If you had adopted this strategy in the early 1980s when interest rates were 15%, then your $500,000 portfolio would have produced a very nice income of $75,000 per year. But as interest rates have declined over the past three decades, the interest income received using this strategy would have also declined - substantially. In late 2009, a 5-year CD was paying only 2.91%, meaning the same $500,000 portfolio would now produce an income of only $14,550.

To compound the problem, inflation has eroded the purchasing power of that $14,550 over the past three decades. Since January of 1981 through late 2009, cumulative inflation has risen almost 150%. That means that your $14,000 worth of income in 2009 can only purchase the same amount of goods and services that $5,800 could purchase in 1981. The cumulative effect of declining interest rates and rising inflation make the interest-only option a long-term losing strategy.

Systematic Withdrawals

The second strategy is to take a systematic withdrawal of a set percentage. As we discussed in Chapter 10, most advisors will agree that 4% is a fairly safe withdrawal rate.

"Now hold on," you may say. "If stocks average 11% and bonds average 5%, why can I take only 4%?" There are two reasons for this. First, because inflation erodes our purchasing power, we need to make sure that we reinvest enough growth back into our portfolio to keep pace with inflation, which has historically averaged around 3.5%. Combined with a 4% withdrawal rate, that means we need to earn 7.5% to both meet our current income needs and keep pace with inflation for the future. Said another way, if we earn 7.5% and withdraw 4%, that allows the principal to grow by 3.5% per year. The next year, our 4% withdrawal will be 3.5% higher due to the growth in principal.

The second reason focuses on our previous discussion of standard deviation and "average return." Even after the two major bear markets of the last decade, as we saw in Table 11.3, the stock market does indeed average around 11% per year. But those averages are made up of widely varying highs and lows, which can dramatically impact the value of your portfolio. We need look no further back than the last ten years to see a great example of this. If we look at the S&P 500 from 1999 to 2008, we see a range of returns from a positive 28.36 to a negative 36.58.

While for a long time the financial services industry emphasized the average return with little more than lip service being paid to the individual variations of each year-by-year return, the market declines of both 2000 and 2008 have taught us that the order in which we receive those returns can make a huge impact on our portfolios.

To illustrate this point, consider the example in Table 11.8. Let's say that you have $100,000 to invest. In Example A you invested that money in a well-balanced portfolio that consistently returned 6.6% per year. At the end of 10 years your initial investment of $100,000 would have grown to $189,484. In Example B, you invested more aggressively and unfortunately suffered losses of -25% and -15% in each of the first two years. After that however, your portfolio starting performing very well and gave you a consistent return of 13.25% for each of the next 8 years, growing your initial $100,000 investment to $172,499. While both portfolios averaged 6.6% over the course of the 10 years, Example A outperformed in the end because it didn't have to make up any losses.

Example A
Initial Investment - $100,000

Year	Return	Yr-End Value
1	6.60%	$ 106,600
2	6.60%	$ 113,636
3	6.60%	$ 121,136
4	6.60%	$ 129,130
5	6.60%	$ 137,653
6	6.60%	$ 146,738
7	6.60%	$ 156,423
8	6.60%	$ 166,747
9	6.60%	$ 177,752
10	6.60%	$ 189,484
Avg Return	6.60%	

Example B
Initial Investment - $100,000

Year	Return	Yr-End Value
1	-25.00%	$ 75,000
2	-15.00%	$ 63,750
3	13.25%	$ 72,197
4	13.25%	$ 81,763
5	13.25%	$ 92,597
6	13.25%	$ 104,866
7	13.25%	$ 118,760
8	13.25%	$ 134,496
9	13.25%	$ 152,317
10	13.25%	$ 172,499
Avg Return	6.60%	

Table 11.8
Comparison of Investment Performance

The point is that negative returns hurt your portfolio far worse than positive returns help it. As such, we must seek to avoid losses at all costs. Rather than investing overly aggressively to maximize returns in the good years, we should seek to invest slightly more conservatively to minimize losses in the bad years. Understanding your portfolio's standard deviation is a good way to try to manage those risks and limit those losses.

The Bucket Strategy

The third withdrawal option is to use the same "bucket" strategy we talked about earlier. Remember that when going through a career or job change, the amounts in your short-term buckets are to be used for immediate living expenses. The same strategy can be applied when you are looking at true retirement.

Using the bucket strategy, four pools of money are created, representing four distinct uses based on your timeframes. The first bucket will contain at least three years of living expenses in very safe, short-term investments. This is the bucket from which you will draw your monthly income. The second bucket will contain another four years worth of living expenses and will be invested in an intermediate-term portfolio. The third bucket will contain one year's worth of living expenses and will be set aside as an emergency investment fund. (I'll explain that more in a minute.) The fourth bucket will include the remainder of your investment assets allocated into a long-term portfolio based on your risk tolerance.

Since living expenses are drawn from the first bucket, this bucket needs to be replenished each year. In years when the stock market and our longer-term portfolio in bucket four does well, we'll withdraw the growth from bucket four to replenish bucket one. In years when bucket four does not do as well, bucket one can be replenished from a combination of withdrawals from buckets two and four. In years when both buckets two and four do poorly, we can replenish from bucket three. By having four years worth of living expenses in safe and secure investments represented by buckets one and three, and an additional four years in intermediate-term investments in bucket two, we have allowed reasonable time for bucket four to recover from the inevitable downturns the stock market is sure to experience.

Annuitize

The fourth and final distribution strategy is to annuitize a portion of your income. Annuities are highly misunderstood investments, so let me try to clear up some of the confusion.

An annuity is a two-phase investment offered by an insurance company. It has an accumulation phase where money is put into the investment as either a lump sum or as periodic contributions over time, and a distribution phase where the money that has been accumulated is paid out as an income to the annuitant (usually the annuity owner, but an annuity can be bought for the benefit of someone else.)

During the accumulation phase, the money that is invested into the annuity can go into either fixed or variable accounts. Just as we discussed earlier, a fixed annuity is similar to putting your money into a CD. It will earn a stated rate of interest and your principal will be guaranteed by the annuity/insurance company. With a variable annuity, you are given the choice of several different mutual-fund-like subaccounts within which to invest your money. (These subaccounts are essentially mutual funds but have slightly different fee structures and other differences, hence a different name.) Most variable annuities (VA's) offer subaccounts up and down the investment risk spectrum so you can create an appropriate asset allocation within the VA. Like mutual funds, you can modify and reallocate money within the VA to meet changing needs or investment strategies. Many annuities offer both fixed and variable investment options within the accumulation phase.

At some point in the future, you will likely want to begin taking money out of the annuity, at which time you have several options. The first option, if the money is invested in a fixed account within the annuity, is to take the interest only. The second option is to take a systematic withdrawal. All the same considerations discussed earlier apply here as well. The third option is to take a partial lump sum. Many annuities have "surrender charges" that apply a fee for early withdrawal. Early could be anywhere from 5-10 years after the initial investment. (We'll talk more about investment fees and charges in the next chapter.) However, many of these same annuities allow you to withdraw a certain percentage of the account - usually around 10% per year - without this surrender penalty. For someone who anticipates just needing occasional access to a small portion of the money, taking as-needed partial lump sum distributions may be the way to go.

One of the common misperceptions about annuities is that the owner loses control of the money. With the three distribution options just mentioned, this is not true. The owner continues to control the money, have access to the money (with potential surrender charges) and can bequest that money to their beneficiaries should they pass away. The only time an annuity owner loses control of the money is if they choose to *annuitize* the annuity. This is both the fourth distribution option within an annuity and the fourth distribution strategy for generating an income.

Annuitizing a portion of one's income helps to solve one of the major problems that most retirees and even "pretirees" may have - not knowing how long we are going to live. One of the biggest fears that retirees have is of outliving their income. What will happen to me if I use up all my money before I die? Annuitizing solves that problem by guaranteeing an income for life. When you choose to annuitize a lump sum of money, the insurance company looks at your age and life expectancy and then calculates how much they can pay you every month for the rest of your life. When you annuitize an annuity, you essentially trade your lump sum of money to the insurance company for a guarantee that they will continue to pay you that monthly amount for the rest of your life, no matter how long you live. Let's look at a quick example.

Let's say you have $160,000 and the insurance company expects you to live 15 years. The insurance company might choose to pay you approximately $1,000 per month. They might be figuring that over that time the $160,000 might earn an additional $20,000 in interest, and therefore $160k +$20k = $180k divided by 180 months (15 years x 12) = $1,000 per month. At the end of those 15 years, theoretically, your $160,000 pool of money should be gone. If, however, you live an additional five years, the insurance/annuity company will continue to pay you that $1,000 month. It's an income you will have for the rest of your life, no matter how long you live. If on the other hand, you die before the original 15 years pass, then the insurance/annuity company will keep whatever is left over in the account.

For many people, annuitizing a lump sum of money is a difficult decision because it has both positive and negative aspects. On the positive side, the peace of mind that comes from knowing they will never be without an income is very welcome. On the negative side, there are two considerations. First, the payments do not usually contain any cost-of-living increase. As we talked about earlier, inflation over 20 years can seriously erode purchasing power and therefore the $1,000 per month that we receive 15 years from now is not likely to support the same standard of living that it does today. Second, the idea that their family would not receive any of the money left in the pool should they die prematurely causes many people to stay away from annuities. In response, most insurance/annuity companies offer "joint life" annuities guaranteeing the income for the lifetime of either spouse, or "period certain" annuities that guarantee a payout for a minimum length of time, regardless of how long the annuitant lives.

One of the biggest advantages that is often overlooked when considering an annuity is the benefit of shared risk. The task of managing your portfolio with both an eye toward long-term growth and immediate generation of income is a considerable challenge. There is no well-defined formula for advisors to follow and very few individual investors have the knowledge necessary to successfully accomplish both. In light of the market declines of the past decade, transferring that risk to an insurance company that can share that risk among a large population is something worth considering for at least some portion of your portfolio.

Chapter 12

Selecting an Advisor

Managing your finances to create financial freedom is not rocket science. It takes an understanding of your attitudes and beliefs about money, a certain amount of knowledge and preparation, and above all - discipline. If you are comfortable doing all these things on your own, I hope this book helps. But if you are not completely comfortable tackling all of this single-handedly, then you may need the help of a financial advisor.

Choosing a financial advisor can be difficult to say the least. At last count there were 48 different designations ranging from Certified Financial Planner (CFP®) and Chartered Financial Consultant (ChFC®) to Accredited Asset Management Specialist (AAMS), Personal Financial Planner (PFP™) and more. It's a regular alphabet soup trying to figure out if the person you're talking to is truly qualified to handle your financial affairs or is really just a glorified salesperson.

Not only do we have to determine if an advisor is competent, but we also have to decide whether we trust them to work in our best interest. While I do believe the vast majority of financial advisors are ethical, the few bad apples who regularly make the news cause us to distrust just about anyone who claims to be able to "help" us handle our money. Coupled with the mortgage, banking and Wall Street bailouts of 2009, the financial services industry in general has done a lousy job of earning, keeping or deserving the public's trust. Nonetheless, we still need them. In this chapter I'll try to shed some light on how the financial advisor industry works and what you should look for when choosing an advisor.

A Rose by Any Other Name...

One of the biggest factors contributing to the public confusion is simply in the titles financial advisors use. Not only are there dozens of designations, but there are also a variety titles including advisor, consultant, representative and agent. While the regulators both require and prohibit the use of certain titles depending on the licenses an advisor may hold, the public has very little understanding of what these different titles mean. Let's start by looking at different titles.

Registered Representative (RR)

A registered representative is someone who has passed one of the Financial Industry Regulatory Authority's (FINRA) various brokerage examination tests and is therefore licensed to buy and sell stocks, bonds, mutual funds and other securities for you. Exactly what they can buy or sell depends on the examination they have passed, the licenses they hold and the firm they work for. Also known as brokers, financial advisors, investment consultants or financial consultants, a registered representative typically earns a commission on the purchase or sale of securities.

It is important to note that just because an RR holds one or more of FINRA's various licenses and is legally able to buy and sell securities, that doesn't mean they have been properly trained as a financial planner. FINRA's examinations are very product oriented. The exams focus on how different investments work, how the markets themselves work, and when various types of investments would be suitable or unsuitable for various investors.

As you can see by all that we've discussed in this book so far, financial planning is a much broader field than just various investments. Figuring out how much you might need for retirement, how much and what types of insurance you should carry or how to budget your expenses are all financial planning topics that FINRA's various exams do not cover. That's why registered representatives will not use the title of financial planner. Unless they have received additional training elsewhere, an RR's primary role is to buy and sell securities.

Investment Advisor

It might sound like the title "investment advisor" is just another term to describe a registered representative, but it is not. An investment advisor is something different altogether. But rather than trying to explain the difference myself, I'll quote FINRA's web site[7]

> *"An investment adviser is an individual or company who is paid for providing advice about securities to their clients. Although the terms sound similar, investment advisers are not the same as financial advisers and should not be confused. The term financial adviser is a generic term that usually refers to a broker (or, to use the technical term, a registered representative).*
>
> *By contrast, the term investment adviser is a legal term that refers to an individual or company that is registered as such with either the Securities and Exchange Commission (SEC) or a state securities regulator. Common names for investment advisers include asset managers, investment counselors, investment managers, portfolio managers, and wealth managers. Investment adviser representatives are individuals who work for and give advice on behalf of registered investment advisers."*

Well that certainly clears things up, doesn't it? Let me try to explain further. Whereas a registered representative's responsibility is focused on a single transaction - the buying or selling of a security - an investment advisor's responsibility is for the management of the money over time. Even though a broker (RR) may conduct a series of transactions over time within an account, each transaction will have its own commission and is looked at as a separate transaction. Further, a registered representative seldom has discretionary authority over an account,

[8] http://www.finra.org/Investors/SmartInvesting/GettingStarted/SelectingInvestmentProfessional/P117278

meaning they cannot buy or sell securities within an account without getting each transaction approved by the client.

An investment advisor on the other hand, will often charge a flat fee (often a percentage of the account balance) to manage the assets in that account. An investment advisor will often have discretionary authority to buy and sell securities within the account based on a pre-agreed upon investment policy statement that outlines the goals, objectives, acceptable investment vehicles, and other particulars, without having to get each transaction individually approved by the client.

Insurance Agent / Broker

An insurance agent is someone who has been licensed to sell insurance products. Just as FINRA provides a licensing exam for securities products, each state has its own insurance commission that tests and licenses individuals to sell insurance products within that state. Again, the types of products an insurance agent can sell depend on the types of licenses the agent holds.

An important distinction needs to be made between an insurance agent and an insurance broker. The term "captive agent" is used to describe someone who sells the products of only one company. While this may be fine, the consumer should know that when working with a captive agent, that agent does not have the ability to provide products from other companies that may be superior to the products the agent's company is offering. An insurance broker or an independent insurance agent have the ability to offer products from a variety of companies and may therefore be able to offer better products as a result.

Financial Planners

Unlike the other professionals, financial planners do not currently have their own regulatory body or licensing requirements. Anyone, as long as they do not infringe into the types of services regulated by FINRA (for registered representatives), the Securities and Exchange Commission or state security commissions (for investment advisors) or state insurance commissions (for insurance agents) can hang out a shingle as a financial planner. In practicality, unless a financial planner's work is limited to budgeting assistance or non-investment-related retirement planning, it's difficult not to infringe on one or more of the regulated areas.

For that reason, most financial planners will carry all of the various licenses and registrations that allow them to act as a registered representative, investment advisor or insurance agent as needed. So once again they have the licenses to conduct business, but do they have the training and expertise?

Of all the designations that are out there and available today, I strongly favor the Certified Financial Planner (CFP®) designation as the one to look for. CFP® certificate holders are required to complete a comprehensive educational requirement that teaches them how to apply the various investment products into real life-planning applications. This educational requirement is typically completed over the course of one to two years, followed by a two-day comprehensive exam, ensuring that applicants actually know the information, not just memorize and regurgitate it for an exam. There is also a three-year experience requirement and continuing education requirements to ensure CFP®s keep up to date on changes in the industry. Finally, the CFP® Board requires each applicant to complete a bi-annual ethics course and commit to a set of practice standards.

Certainly there are bad apples within the ranks of CFP®s as well, but the stringent requirements of receiving and maintaining that designation tend to weed out a majority of those who might be tempted to take shortcuts with either their knowledge or ethics.

Understanding Fees

Within the financial services industry, advisors get paid in primarily three different ways - by commission, through fees based on assets under management or through fees based on services rendered. Let's look at each one.

Commissions

In the old days when "full service" brokerage firms were the only real option for purchasing stocks, bonds or mutual funds, commissions of 8.5% or more were not uncommon. But with the rise of online trading and the surge in mutual fund popularity in the 80s and 90s, most of these full-service firms have changed to a "Fee for Assets Under Management" model, which we'll discuss in a few minutes. That means that today a large percentage of stock transactions are done for minimal fees of less than $20 through one of the various online brokerage firms like Charles Schwab, E*Trade or TD Ameritrade. With mutual funds continuing to dominate the market as the most common investment vehicle for the majority of Americans, let's start with an explanation of not just the commissions charged by mutual funds, but the whole mutual fund expense picture.

Investors today have four basic fee structures under which they can purchase a mutual fund. These are called a Front-End Load (known as A-shares), a Back-End Load (known as B-shares), a Level-Load (known as C-shares) and a No-Load. The word "load" refers to a sales commission.

On a front-loaded fund, the fund will typically charge a 5% fee (it could range anywhere from 1% to 5.75%, but is usually around 5%[8]) right up front just to put the money into the fund. That means that if you invest $10,000 into the fund, the fund will take $500 right up front as a sales charge, and will invest only $9,500 into your account.

With a back-end loaded fund, there is no fee to put the money in, but your money is subject to a multiyear declining surrender charge - i.e. a penalty for early withdrawal. This fee is referred to as a Contingent Deferred Sales Charge (CDSC), and typically starts at 5% for withdrawals made within the first year and then declines over six years so that at the end of the sixth full year, there is no charge to take the money out. The surrender schedule can vary both the number of years and the percentage charged each year, but often follows the schedule illustrated in Table 12.1.

[8] Most front-end loaded funds offer discounts called breakpoints (a reduced charge for larger investment amounts) and "rights of accumulation" (again a reduced charge based on the total amount an investor has with that fund company in different accounts.) These discounts typically start at around $50,000 and can potentially reduce the front-end load to zero for investments of $1 million or more.

A level-load fund, like a back-end load, charges no fee to get in, but instead of having a six- or seven-year surrender period, it typically has only a one-year surrender period, during which time the surrender penalty is only 1%. After one year, there is no fee to take the money out. With a no-load fund, there is no fee to put the money in or take the money out at any time. A comparison of the various load options is shown in Table 12.1.

	Front End Load (A)	Back End Load (B)	Level Load (C)	No Load
Sales Commission	5% Up front	0% Up front Yr. CDSC 1 5% 2 4% 3 3% 4 3% 5 2% 6 1% 7+ 0%	0% Up front Yr. CDSC 1 1% 2+ 0%	0% any time

Table 12.1
Common Mutual Fund Load Options

If this were all there was to it, the choice would be fairly simple - of course we'd go with a no-load fund that doesn't charge any sales commissions at any time. Unfortunately that's not all there is to it. In addition to a sales commission, all mutual funds charge an ongoing expense ratio. Rather than being a one-time charge like the sales load, the annual expense ratio is built into the price of the fund and essentially subtracted from the net asset value (price) of the fund every single day. If, for example, a mutual fund had an expense ratio of 1%, then the fund would charge essentially 1/365th of 1% every day when it calculated the fund's share price. In this way the expense ratio is invisible, but just like a sales load, it directly impacts the value and return of the fund.

Because this expense ratio is invisible, many no-load investors mistakenly believe that they are charged nothing for the management of their money within the fund. Not only is this not true, it doesn't make sense. Would you work for free? Why then would we expect our no-load mutual fund company to do so? The fact is *every* mutual fund out there charges for their services in the form of an expense ratio. As we'll see in moment, however, some charge significantly more than others.

The last thing to mention about mutual fund expense ratios is that the total expense ratio is made up of various other individual charges. These charges include:

- ❖ A management fee to pay the managers who are actually making the buy and sell decisions within the fund (per the actively-managed fund discussion in Chapters 9 and 11).
- ❖ Administration charges for accounting, recordkeeping, customer services and the like.
- ❖ A 12b-1 fee. The 12b-1 fee is often singled out as a particularly distasteful fee because it is referred to as a "marketing distribution expense." Essentially the 12b-1 fee is additional commission paid out to the brokerage firm to compensate a registered representative for ongoing servicing of the account. As we'll discuss in a moment, if you rarely contact your registered representative then this is an expense you'll want to avoid. But if you have consistent contact with your rep, then it provides a way to compensate that individual for the service they provide.

For most front-end loaded funds a typical expense ratio is around .75% - 1%. It may be higher or lower than that range but this is typical. How that annual expense is broken down among management fees, administration expense and 12b-1 fees varies from fund to fund and is not overly important, other than to say those funds without 12b-1 fees are typically on the lower end of the range.

For back-end loaded funds, since there is no up-front load, the annual expense ratio is typically quite a bit higher, generally anywhere from 1.5% to 2% or more. One of the best ways to understand this is to compare it to buying points on a mortgage. When you take out a home mortgage, you are often given the option to buy down your interest rate by purchasing "points." When you buy points, you essentially pay a lump sum of money up front in order to lower the interest rate on your loan. The logic is that over the life of a 30-year loan, you'll save back what you paid up front as a lump sum through lower monthly payments. If you plan on having that mortgage for a long time, then it is often a good move to purchase points. If however, you plan on holding that mortgage for only a short while, you probably won't have time to make up the initial outlay.

The same strategy is true for mutual funds. If you plan on holding the fund for a long timeframe, paying a front-end load (the analogy equivalent of points) along with lower annual expenses (the analogy equivalent of the interest rate) may actually cost less than not paying an up-front load but being subjected to a higher annual expense ratio. The longer you plan on holding the fund, the more important a low expense ratio becomes.

For level-loaded funds, the expense ratio is often the same as for back-end loaded funds. Again, since you didn't pay anything up front, the annual expense will typically be higher. The only difference between back-end loaded funds and level-loaded funds is that the expense ratio for a back-end loaded fund will revert to the expense ratio of a front-end loaded fund typically one year after the surrender period ends. In this way the investor is not stuck with that higher expense ratio forever. As you might surmise, the term "level load" comes from the fact that this higher expense ratio remains in place throughout the length of time you hold the fund.

With a no-load fund, the annual expenses can vary dramatically. In the case of passively-managed index funds, the expense ratio can be .2% (2/10ths of 1%) or less, while actively-managed aggressive funds can be 2% or more. The typical no-load mutual fund total expense ratio is often around .75%.

To get a clear picture of what the true costs of a mutual fund are, you need to look at both the load and the expense ratio over the length of time you expect to hold the fund. If for example, you plan on holding that mutual fund for five years, the total costs of a front-end loaded fund with a 5% load and 1% annual expense ratio would be approximately 10% total over those five years. (Calculated by taking 5% + {1% x 5 years} = 10%.) A comparison example of total costs for each share class over 5 years using our typical figures is illustrated in Table 12.2.

	Front End Load (A)	Back End Load (B)	Level Load (C)	No Load
Sales Commission	5% Up front	0% Up front Yr CDSC 1 5% 2 4% 3 3% 4 3% 5 2% 6 1% 7+ 0%	0% Up front Yr CDSC 1 1% 2+ 0%	0% any time
Annual Expense Ratio	Typically .75% to 1%	1.5% - 2+% (Typically reverts to .75% to 1% 1 year after the CDSC period ends.)	1.5% - 2+%	.2 - 2% (Typically Around .75%)
Five Years Annual Expense Ratio	5 yrs x 1% = 5%	5 yrs x 2% = 10%	5 yrs x 2% = 10%	5 yrs x .75% = 3.75%
Total Cost Over Five Years (Sales Commission Plus Annual Expenses)	10%	12%	10%	3.75%

Table 12.2
Comparison of Mutual Fund Costs

As you can see, they all get paid someplace. If the no-load fund you choose has an annual expense ratio closer to the high end of the range around 2%, then your total cost for that fund over five years would be right around the same 10% total as for the other choices.

Don't feel bad if you find this confusing or get intimidated thinking you'll have to make all these calculations yourself. Thankfully, FINRA has created an online calculator where you can compare various funds and receive an interactive report that illustrates the projected total costs and impact those costs will have on your investment. The calculator can be found at http://apps.finra.org/fundanalyzer/1/fa.aspx.

Based on the typical expense ratios and time-weighted impact those expenses will have on your investment, it becomes fairly clear that for the most part, no-load funds are indeed less expensive than loaded funds. With that being the case, why would anyone ever buy a loaded fund? The answer comes in asking another question, which is, "What do you get for the load that you pay?"

Mutual fund loads do one thing and one thing only - they pay for the help of a financial advisor. A large portion of the load you pay goes back to the brokerage firm in the form of a "dealer concession" (a.k.a. - commission) that is typically split between the advisor and the firm. This is not a bad thing *if* you received real assistance from your advisor. That's what it all boils down to. If your advisor took the time to understand your needs, answer your questions and put together an overall plan that addressed not just the immediate financial need, but also worked with you to develop a solution that would meet your long-term life goals, then like any professional they should be compensated for their services. Commissions are one way to do that. If, on the other hand, they just quickly recommended the "fund of the day" without really trying to understand your goals and risk tolerance, then that is probably not an advisor with whom you want to have a long-term relationship.

No-load funds are for those investors who want to invest on their own, without the help of a financial advisor. If that's you, then go for it. As we've discussed throughout this book, creating financial freedom is not rocket science. Any of us are capable of learning what we need to know to create a financial plan and begin investing on our own. BUT - and this is a big but - there are three big reasons why you might want to work with an advisor.

First, most of us don't have the time, energy or inclination to do all the initial and ongoing research on our own. Managing investments as well as staying abreast of ever-changing tax laws and financial planning trends is a full-time job. As mentioned earlier, many financial planners will carry one or more FINRA licenses, insurance licenses, and SEC Investment Advisor licenses. Coupled with that, considering the initial and ongoing continuing education to become a CFP®, it is just not realistic to think that someone with a full-time job (or having full-time fun!) can gain and maintain the same level of knowledge that a professional financial advisor can.

Second, as we discussed earlier, money can be a very emotional subject. While in times of relative market calm, we all believe that we'll act rationally when the markets inevitably become volatile. But when irrational behavior takes over the market and we are alone late at night trying to decide whether to stay in or jump out, irrational decisions suddenly seem very logical. Especially when we are talking about our own money that we'll use to fund our own hopes and dreams, it's virtually impossible to maintain a level head. Having a financial advisor who understands our hopes and dreams is very helpful in keeping us on track and making the decisions that will give us the best chance of achieving those dreams.

Finally, when it comes to making investment decisions, experience counts. And not just experience in number of years, but experience with various situations. When you are investing on your own you have one portfolio, and therefore one chance to consistently make the right decisions. A financial advisor who has been in the industry for a number of years has seen different markets, and has experience with hundreds of different client portfolios. They know how to build portfolios that withstand various market conditions. That experience is invaluable when it comes time to make those tough decisions.

Mutual funds are obviously not the only product that charge commissions, but the fee structures for mutual funds are easily applied to other types of products. Fixed and variable annuities, for instance, often have fee structures very similar to back-end loaded, level-load, or no-load mutual funds.

While investors have always had a distrust of advisors who receive commissions, I can tell you that I have known hundreds of very good, very ethical advisors who earned their living based on commissions, as well as from fees for assets under management or services rendered. I have also known advisors who received their compensation in all three ways who, to put it mildly, couldn't plan their way out of a paper bag. The key is to find an advisor who is competent and knowledgeable, one who is able to provide services in accordance with the investment philosophy that you desire, who is also ethical, caring and takes the time to put you, not just your money, at the center of the relationship. These traits are far more important than whether or not they receive commissions.

Asset Under Management (AUM) Fees

Even though there are many good, ethical, commission-based advisors out there, many investors (as well as many advisors) are simply not comfortable with compensating their financial advisor in that way. As a result, many advisors have turned to charging fees for assets under management.

Whereas an advisor must hold one of FINRA's registered representative licenses in order to receive commissions, that same advisor must also be registered with either the SEC or one of the individual state's securities departments as a Registered Investment Advisor or Investment Advisor Representative to receive fees for assets under management. Often this requires obtaining additional licenses from FINRA in order to register with the SEC or the various states, but other designations, including the CFP®, will also permit an individual to register. If they are not registered, they cannot charge asset under management fees.

In this fee structure, an advisor will often use no-load mutual funds, ETFs or even individual stocks or bonds to create an investment portfolio for the client, and will then charge a separate fee for those services. That fee can range from as low as ½ of 1% to 2% or more. Typically this fee will be around 1% each year.

When you look at what's happening here, it's really not all that different from a level-loaded mutual fund. The higher expense ratio of back-end loaded and level-loaded mutual funds is due in large part to a higher 12b-1 fee, which compensates the financial advisor for ongoing servicing of the account. In a fee for assets under management arrangement, rather than charging the fee at the mutual-fund level, virtually the same fee is assessed separately by the advisor. The only real difference is the visibility of the fee. As mentioned, in a mutual fund that fee is invisible because it is built into the price of the fund. In a fee for assets under management arrangement, the fee is typically assessed quarterly and is deducted directly from the account.

Again, one of the biggest questions an investor should ask themselves when it comes to this or any type of fee arrangement, is "What am I getting for the fee that I pay?" This is a good time to further clarify the roles that the various parties within the financial services industry play.

A good financial advisor is one who focuses on you and your goals. This person should understand tax planning, retirement planning, education funding, insurance planning, budgeting and other financial planning concepts, not just investments. They then use their knowledge of various financial concepts and investment products to recommend investments and strategies that will help you achieve your goals. They should not be "managing" the money themselves.

The fact is that managing money by selecting individual stocks or bonds is a very different job than being a financial planner or financial advisor. Whereas a financial advisor will provide planning around several different topics, they will also help you create an overall asset allocation for your investments. A money manager on the other hand, is only concerned about that portion of the allocation they manage. An advisor may suggest using three different managers to handle the stock portion of your portfolio. When doing so, the advisor is then turning over the actual buy-and-sell decisions for the individual stocks that make up that portion of your portfolio to the money manager. That's a good thing.

A money manager doesn't spend his days talking to individual clients like a financial advisor does, they talk to corporate chief financial officers (CFOs) and chief executive officers (CEOs). They analyze the books of a company using fundamental analysis and then look at trading patterns using technical analysis to try to determine how they can add the most value to that specific asset category. Money managers don't necessarily care about your individual goals; they manage money with a certain philosophy to meet a certain goal. If your goal matches theirs, great; but they are not concerned about your overall asset allocation. They are concerned only about the portion of your asset allocation that they manage.

When it comes to fees then, both the advisor and the manager need to be paid. In a mutual fund, the advisor is paid with a load (and potentially a 12b-1 fee) while the manager is paid through the management fees as part of the annual expense ratio. In a fee for assets under management arrangement, the manager and advisor are paid separately. The advisor's fee is deducted directly from the account. Depending on the investment vehicles chosen by the advisor, the manager's fees may be built into the no-load funds or ETFs the advisor has chosen, or they may be charged as an additional separate account management fee.

In some cases, in order to control costs or because an advisor believes that the active management of a money manager does not add significant value, the advisor will act as both advisor and money manager. In this case the advisor will typically use ETFs or index funds to implement their asset allocation strategy. While some advisors are very successful playing both roles, they typically have a large support team as it is a very big job. Make sure you know what role your advisor is playing and if they are using outside money managers or attempting to fill both roles themselves.

Fees for Services Rendered

Because managing money and being a financial advisor are such different roles, some financial advisors choose to clearly distinguish between the two by separately charging for the planning services they provide. Much like an accountant or attorney will charge for their services, in a fee-for-services-rendered arrangement the client is now paying purely for the advisor's time and planning advice. This charge can take the form of an hourly rate ranging from $100 to $500 per hour or more, to a project rate up into the thousands of dollars for retirement, estate and tax planning services. Some fee-for-service advisors offer retainer packages to their clients to provide ongoing, year-round access.

While some advisors will charge both service fees and commissions or AUM fees, many fee-for-service advisors choose to forego all other types of compensation and charge strictly for the planning advice they offer. The feeling is that this allows them to be completely objective and to avoid any potential conflicts of interest as they do not handle brokerage or investment advisory accounts at all. Typically a fee-for-service advisor will refer their clients to two or three different discount brokerage houses and have the client establish the accounts there, without direct involvement from the advisor. The advisor will instruct clients on a given asset allocation and may then allow clients to select the specific investments that will fulfill the asset allocation.

In addition to objectivity, the other significant advantage of a fee-for-service type of arrangement includes complete transparency of fees - clients know exactly how much they are paying and what they are receiving for their money. The largest disadvantage is that investors are required to implement the advice on their own. Depending on the help an advisor provides, navigating the paperwork maze of opening brokerage accounts, transferring assets and keeping their own records in order can be a nuisance. Without someone doing this for them, many investors simply procrastinate and end up failing to implement the plan.

Salaried Financial Advisors

Some advisors receive a salary from their employer, either as their sole compensation or as a base salary with bonuses. Usually that salary is funded by some combination of commissions, AUM fees or fees for services rendered that are then charged by or paid to their employer.

What to Look for When Selecting an Advisor

As you can see, there are lots of different types of financial advisors out there who offer a wide range of services and charge for their services in a variety of ways. How do you find one who's right for you?

The first place to start is to determine exactly what it is you need:

- Are you a do-it-yourself investor who wants only a professional opinion to confirm you're on the right track? (If so, a fee-for-service advisor might be the right choice.)

- Do you want someone to handle all of your financial affairs for you? (Then a financial planner/investment advisor might be the way to go.)

- Do you need comprehensive planning advice? (Then you may need a CFP®.)

- Are you looking for just a quick investment recommendation? (Then consider working through a registered representative.)

The second thing you should be clear on is how you want your money managed - strategically, tactically or by using a hybrid approach. An investor who expects to receive phone calls advising them when to move into and out of the market will be sorely disappointed by an advisor who utilizes a strategic "buy and hold" approach. At the same time, an investor who wants to "set it and forget it" will be frustrated by an advisor who takes a more active, tactical approach.

You should also understand your own money personality - do you tend to lean more towards being an Eagle or a Condor? Financial Eagles may be better served by working with a more conservative advisor to balance out their aggressive Eagle tendencies. And while finding an advisor you can relate to is important to both money personalities, it is especially important to the financial Condor.

Once you know these things about yourself, you are now ready to look for an advisor. I recommend interviewing several advisors before settling on any one. When interviewing an advisor, there are several questions you should ask:

1. How long has the advisor been in the business and what experience do they have? Find out how long the planner has been in practice and how many firms have they been associated with. Ask the planner to briefly describe their work experience and how it relates to their current practice.

2. Find out what professional designations or licenses they hold. More is not always better, but they should have at least a couple. For registered representatives a FINRA Series 6 or Series 7, along with a Series 63 are minimum requirements. A Registered Investment Advisor or Investment Advisor Representative should hold either a FINRA Series 65 or 66, or have a professional designation such as CFP®, Chartered Financial Analyst (CFA), Personal Financial Specialist (PFS), Charter Financial Consultant (ChFC) or Chartered Investment Counselor (CIC). Any advisor who sells insurance or annuity products must also hold appropriate state insurance licenses. Again, I recommend working with someone who has attained the CFP® designation.

3. Do they belong to any professional organizations? The financial services industry has several member support organizations including the Financial Planning Association (FPA) and the National Association of Personal Financial Advisors (NAPFA.) Membership in any of these organizations does not assure competence, but it indicates that the advisor takes their profession seriously as a career, not just as a job.

4. What services do they offer? Do they provide comprehensive financial planning, insurance and investments? Or do they specialize in just one facet of the industry? Do they act as both financial advisor and money manager, or do they outsource any portion of their services?

5. What is their approach to the client relationship? How will they provide ongoing service to you?

6. What approach do they take to investing? Strategic, tactical or a hybrid approach?

7. What kind of support team do they have? Are they a small, one-person independent shop, or do they have multiple team members who will also work with you?

8. Who are their significant business support partners? This may be a brokerage firm, Registered Investment Advisor, insurance agency or other money managers and vendors they work with.

9. How will you pay for their services? Do they receive commissions, charge for services rendered, or assess a fee for assets under management? What is a typical fee schedule?

10. Do they use an agreement that defines the scope and responsibilities of the client-advisor relationship? While almost all investment advisors and fee-for-service advisors will have some type of client agreement, very few registered representatives currently do so. Again, it is not a requirement, but an agreement does a good job of getting in writing exactly what each party is responsible for and can help to avoid mismatched expectations later in the relationship.

11. Check the various regulatory web sites to determine if the advisor has had any regulatory actions taken against them. Several sites you should check include:

- For FINRA registered representatives utilize FINRA's BrokerCheck at http://www.finra.org/Investors/ToolsCalculators/BrokerCheck/index.htm

- For Investment Advisors you can use the SEC's Investment Advisor Public Disclosure search at http://www.adviserinfo.sec.gov/IAPD/Content/Search/iapd_OrgSearch.aspx. Note: You should also check with your state securities regulators as many advisors are registered with individual states, not the SEC.

- Even though the CFP Board that oversees the activities of Certified Financial Planners is not a regulatory body, it does protect the use of its marks and will issue disciplinary actions against advisors who fail to meet the competency or ethical requirements set forth by the Board. Investors can check to see if the CFP Advisor they are interviewing has been the subject of any CFP Board disciplinary action by going to http://www.cfp.net/search/.

Once you have interviewed several advisors, you should be able to get a feel for their approach and determine if their style is appropriate for you. Do they seem interested in getting to know you? Do they answer your questions directly and without hesitation? Do you feel they are being honest and truthful? Most advisors that you would want to work with will welcome the opportunity to get to know you before diving into the planning process. One big red flag is that if the advisor starts talking about products and investments (other than to explain the services they offer) before asking a number of questions about you, that is probably someone you want to avoid.

Financial Life Planning

As we've talked throughout this book, the idea that financial planning is just about numbers and investments isn't in touch with the social trends of today. Throughout the world there is a growing trend toward personal awakening - the idea that each of us has a purpose and that we should find and express that purpose in our lives.

Out of this trend (or perhaps leading this trend) is an emerging niche within the financial planning industry called financial life planning. Financial life planning recognizes the importance of both money and purpose in our lives and recognizes that financial planning should do more than just help you become financially independent - it should help you achieve your deepest, most heartfelt life goals.

The fact of the matter is however, that this softer side of financial planning has yet to be widely embraced by the financial planning community. Most advisors have enough on their plates just keeping up with ever-changing tax laws, investment regulation and the hard skills associated with the financial planning profession. Add to that the fact that most in the financial services industry simply tend to be more left brain, logical, numbers-oriented individuals, while financial life planning requires a more right-brain, relationship-oriented approach, it's not hard to see why adoption has been slow. While there are several organizations out there who train financial advisors on these life planning issues most advisors are neither qualified nor comfortable in having these deeper, more life purpose-oriented kinds of conversations with their clients.

Not only are advisors often uncomfortable with these conversations, but so too are many clients. We rarely divulge our deepest life goals and dreams to even the most trusted individuals in our lives. Several advisors who have been trained in financial life planning report that it often takes a year or more before clients finally feel comfortable enough to truly open up.

That's why in addition to this book, I've created the Retirement 20/20™ Life Planning Profile. Located at Retirement2020.com, the

Life Planning Profile is a 90-question assessment covering the Six Key Life Arenas discussed earlier. The assessment produces an 18-page report including suggested action items to help you begin to create the life you want. The report is also a useful tool that can help you initiate these kinds of life planning conversations with your advisor so that you can assure your financial plan also meets your life plan.

Summary

As I look back at my own life and the lives of so many clients I've worked with over the years, I realize that creating the life you want requires you overcome both financial and psychological obstacles. We have to give ourselves permission to dream, permission to challenge conventional thinking and permission to do what we truly want to do right now. I hope that this book helps you to define what your ideal life looks like, remove the psychological obstacles that prevent you from moving forward and provide the tools and knowledge you need to begin creating the life you want today.

About the Author

Keith J. Weber, CFP®

Keith J Weber spent 20 years in the financial services industry. During that time he watched hundreds of clients struggle with the daily disillusionment of their jobs while in pursuit of the retirement dream.

Now as a speaker, author, coach and consultant, Keith helps individuals and organziations reignite their passion for work and life. Keith continues to hold the CERTIFIED FINANCIAL PLANNER™ certification and is a Certified Professional Retirement Coach.

Appendices

Appendix 1

Dreams Exercise

Write out the particulars of your dreams in as much detail as possible. Include the people you are with, the setting or environment you're in, what you are doing and what makes this dream so meaningful to you. What is it about this dream that really gets you excited? Do this for each of your dreams and feel free to use additional paper if necessary.

Dream #1

Dream #2

Dream #3

Common Themes Among My Dreams

Appendix 2

Identify Your Values Exercise

Step 1

Examine the list below. Select 10-12 (or more) words or phrases that have particularly strong meaning to you and represent ideals that are personally important to you. Try to filter out any external voices in your head that try to tell you what you "should" select. Instead, listen to your inner voice and select those that feel right to you. Feel free to include any others that are important to you but not on the list.

Accomplishment	Fairness	Moral
Achievement	Faith / Spirituality	Optimism
Adaptability	Family	Power
Authority	Freedom	Prestige
Autonomy/Independence	Friendships	Purpose
Beauty	Growth	Recognition
Challenge	Health	Respect
Compensation	Helping Others Individually	Responsibility
Competition	Helping Society	Risk
Control	Honesty	Safety
Cooperation/Teamwork	Humility	Security
Creativity	Integrity	Selflessness
Diversity	Justice	Service
Enjoyment / Fun	Knowledge	Status
Ethical	Leadership	Trust
Excitement	Love	Variety
Expertise	Loyalty	Wealth
Exploration/Discovery	Meaning	

Step 2

In the space below or on a separate piece of paper, write out a brief description of what each of your selected values mean to you. Again, filter out any voices that tell you how you "should" define these values and create a definition that's personally meaningful to you. It doesn't have to be a long or grammatically correct definition, just a description of what that value means to you.

My Values

1. ______________________________
2. ______________________________
3. ______________________________
4. ______________________________
5. ______________________________
6. ______________________________
7. ______________________________
8. ______________________________
9. ______________________________
10. ______________________________
11. ______________________________
12. ______________________________

Step 3

Prioritize your values by selecting the five most important. Try to think back on experiences where the values were either upheld or compromised. How important was it to you that the value was treated in that way? Those that create the most powerful feelings are your most important values.

My Top Five Values

1. ____
2. ____
3. ____
4. ____
5. ____

Step 4

Sleep on it. Put your list aside for a few days and then come back to it and review it. Are your top five still the most important? Make changes if necessary and come back to it every few days until you feel the list is solid.

Step 5

Commit to them. Now that you know what your values are, be consciously aware of situations and circumstances that will allow you to live and promote your values, and be wary of those situations that ask you to compromise your values.

Knowing your values will help provide the guidance to make tough decisions between competing priorities. The best definition of stress that I have ever come across is that "Stress occurs when your actions are inconsistent with your values and beliefs." Sometimes in our work and in other areas of our lives we are often asked to do things that don't seem right. By knowing our values and making a commitment to live them, we can eliminate much of the stress and pressure in our lives.

Appendix 3

Interests and Activities Exercise

In the space provided, enter the interests and activities that fulfill the stated criteria.

Interests / Activities that I currently enjoy

1. ______________________________
2. ______________________________
3. ______________________________
4. ______________________________
5. ______________________________

Interests / Activities I used to enjoy

1. ______________________________
2. ______________________________
3. ______________________________
4. ______________________________
5. ______________________________

Interests / Activities I have always wanted to pursue

1. ______________________________
2. ______________________________
3. ______________________________
4. ______________________________
5. ______________________________

Interests / Activities that will keep me physically active

1. ______________________________
2. ______________________________
3. ______________________________
4. ______________________________
5. ______________________________

Interests / Activities that will help me grow personally or spiritually

1. ______________________________
2. ______________________________
3. ______________________________
4. ______________________________
5. ______________________________

Interests / Activities that I can share with those who are closest to me

1. ______________________________
2. ______________________________
3. ______________________________
4. ______________________________
5. ______________________________

Interests / Activities that will keep me mentally engaged and challenged

1. ______________________________
2. ______________________________
3. ______________________________
4. ______________________________
5. ______________________________

Interests / Activities that will help me pursue a meaningful purpose

1. ______________________________
2. ______________________________
3. ______________________________
4. ______________________________
5. ______________________________

Interests / Activities that I may use to earn income

1. ______________________________
2. ______________________________
3. ______________________________
4. ______________________________
5. ______________________________

Interests / Activities that I can share with friends

1. ______________________________
2. ______________________________
3. ______________________________
4. ______________________________
5. ______________________________

Look back at each list and select the 10-15 that are most important to you. They may include the most meaningful or even those that are easiest to achieve. Look for ways to start integrating these activities into your life.

My Top Interests / Activities

1. ____
2. ____
3. ____
4. ____
5. ____
6. ____
7. ____
8. ____

4\. ____

10\. ____

11\. ____

12\. ____

13\. ____

14\. ____

15\. ____

Appendix 4

Eagle and Condor Beliefs

Money is the root of all evil - Condor

A penny saved is a penny earned. - Eagle

Money doesn't grow on trees. - Eagle

If you have everything you want, others won't have enough. - Condor

Talking about money is in poor taste. - Condor

Wealthy people are dishonest. - Condor

Money is a scorecard - more is better. - Eagle

Save your money for a rainy day. - Eagle

Money only comes to those who work hard. - Eagle

Carpe diem! Live for today! - Condor

Money is fair, it goes to those who earn it. - Eagle

The system is built so the rich get richer. - Condor

RECOMMENDED READING

(ALL BOOKS AVAILABLE ON EARLYRETIREMENTHELP.COM)

Work Less, Live More
Bob Clyatt
For those who want to retire real early, Work Less, Live More provides practical tips on how to cut expenses and structure investment portfolios so you can take back your time by living off the income from part-time work. **ISBN: 1413307051**

How to Retire Happy, Wild and Free
Ernie J. Zelinski
Recognizing that many of us equate "who we are" with "what we do", author Ernie Zelinski helps readers create a new identity for themselves after retirement by focusing on how to find purposeful and meaningful activities after retiring. **ISBN: 1580085784**

Retire Happy
Rich Stim and Ralph Warner
Authors Rich Stim and Ralph Warner look beyond just the financial aspects of retirement to provide insight on what's really important in life. Referencing a wealth of survey data from USAToday, the authors show how you can begin to prepare yourself both financially and emotionally for the transition into retirement. **ISBN: 141330835X**

Solving the Retirement Puzzle
J. Peter Lindquist
This is a great book detailing the experiences of 40 different individuals who have transitioned into retirement. Some have done so very successfully, while others have faced struggles that have come from a variety of circumstances. Throughout the book, Lindquist uses these real-life stories as both warnings and lessons that retirement happiness doesn't always come in ways you expect. **ISBN: 0972342222**

What Color is Your Parachute? For Retirement
Richard Bolles and John E. Nelson

Using a holistic "life planning" approach, authors Bolles and Nelson examine various life elements including your family and social relationships, psychological strengths and geographic preferences to help you construct an ideal retirement. **ISBN: 1580087116**

The Joy of Not Working: A Book for the Retired, Unemployed, and Overworked
Ernie J. Zelinski

A textbook for those who want to live life to the fullest, The Joy of Not Working shows you how create a satisfying work/life balance by working less, producing more and gaining the courage to leave a life-draining job. **ISBN: 1580085520**

The Soul of Money
Lynne Twist

This inspirational book helps us examine our own attitudes and beliefs about money, and how those beliefs may be standing in the way of our achieving the peace, happiness and security we really want. Highly recommended for anyone who suffers anxiety over money, this book teaches us how to put money into it's proper perspective in our lives. **ISBN: 039332950X**

The Richest Man in Babylon
George S. Clason

A personal finance classic! This simple book effectively teaches the timeless fundamentals of acquiring money, keeping money and making our money earn more money. In today's world we often forget the basics. This great book reminds us of the basic rules of what we need to do to be financially successful.**ISBN: 0451205367**

The Truth About Money
Ric Edelman

For more details on everything from insurance to investments, mortgages and home purchases, even retirement and estate planning, this book is a great resource of easy-to-understand information on virtually every aspect of personal finance.
ISBN: 0060566582

Escape from Corporate America: A Practical Guide to Creating the Career of Your Dreams
Pamela Skillings
Early retirement today doesn't mean you'll never work again, it often means you'll simply stop doing work you no longer enjoy. Escape from Corporate America provides a step-by-step guide to help you discover the kind of work you really want to do, and how to develop your "escape plan" so you can create the life you really want. **ISBN: 0345499743**

For the more academic:

Beyond Greed and Fear: Understanding Behavioral Finance and the Psychology of Investing
by Hersh Shefrin **ISBN: 0195161211**

Toward a Psychology of Being, 3rd Edition
by Abraham H. Maslow **ISBN: 0471293091**

RESOURCES

Books:

Behavioral Finance and Wealth Management: How to Build Optimal Portfolios That Account for Investor Biases
by Michael M Pompian ISBN: 0471745170

Better than Good: Creating a Life You Can't Wait to Live
by Zig Ziglar ISBN: 159145400X

Beyond Greed and Fear: Understanding Behavioral Finance and the Psychology of Investing
by Hersh Shefrin ISBN: 0195161211

Career Coaching: An Insider's Guide
by Marcia Bench ISBN: 0891061843

Escape from Corporate America: A Practical Guide to Creating the Career of Your Dreams
by Pamela Skillings ISBN: 0345499743

How to Retire Happy, Wild and Free
by Ernie J. Zelinski ISBN: 1580085784

Solving the Retirement Puzzle
by J. Peter Lindquist ISBN: 0972342222

Snap Judgment: When to Trust Your Instincts, When to Ignore Them, and How to Avoid Making Big Mistakes with Your Money
by David E. Adler ISBN: 9780137147786

Total Life Coaching
by Patrick William and Lloyd J. Thomas ISBN: 0393704343

Toward a Psychology of Being, 3rd Edition
by Abraham H. Maslow ISBN: 0471293091

The Truth About Money
by Ric Edelman ISBN: 0060566582

What Color is Your Parachute? For Retirement
by Richard N. Bolles and John E Nelson ISBN: 1580087116

Work Less, Live More
by Bob Clyatt ISBN: 1413307051

Articles/Papers:

2007-2008 Global Workforce Study
Towers Perrin (TowersWatson) HR Services
Available online at
http://www.towersperrin.com/tp/showhtml.jsp?url=global/publications/gws/index.htm&country=global

2008 National Study of Employers
Families and Work Institute
Available online at
http://www.familiesandwork.org/site/research/reports/2008nse.pdf

The 2009 Annual Report of the Board of Trustees of the Federal Old-Age and Survivors Insurance and Federal Disability Insurance Trust Funds
Available online at http://www.ssa.gov/OACT/TR/2009/

The 2010 Consumer Financial Literacy Survey Final Report
National Foundation for Credit Counseling
Available online at
http://www.nfcc.org/Newsroom/FinancialLiteracy/files2010/2010ConsumerFinancialLiteracySurveyFinalReport.pdf

The CitiSales Study of Older Workers, November, 2008
The Sloan Center on Aging & Work at Boston College
Available online at **http://www.uky.edu/Centers/iwin/citisales/**

The Consumer Expenditure Survey
US Department of Labor Bureau of Labor Statistics
Available online at **http://www.bls.gov/cex/csxann08.pdf**

EBRI Issue Brief No. 304, April 2007
Available online at
http://www.ebri.org/pdf/briefspdf/EBRI_IB_04a-20075.pdf

The Financial Crisis and Private Defined Benefit Plans, November, 2008
Center for Retirement Research at Boston College
Available online at
http://crr.bc.edu/briefs/the_financial_crisis_and_private_defined_benefit_plans_2.html

The Financial Crisis and State/Local Defined Benefit Plans, November, 2008
Center for Retirement Research at Boston College
Available online at
http://crr.bc.edu/index.php?option=com_content&task=emailform&id=636

From Materialist to Postmaterialist Happiness? World Values Research Vol 2 / Num 2 / 2009
World Values Survey
Available online at **http://www.worldvaluessurvey.org/**

Recent Trends in Household Wealth in the United States: Rising Debt and the Middle-Class Squeeze, June 2007
Edward N Wolff, The Levy Economics Institute of Bard College and Department of Economics, New York University
Available online at **http://www.levyinstitute.org/pubs/wp_502.pdf**

Satisfaction and Engagement in Retirement, July 2005
Urban Institute
Available online at
http://www.urban.org/publications/311202.html

A Theory of Human Motivation
A. H. Maslow (1943)
Originally Published in Psychological Review, 50, 370-396

Websites:

AARP
www.aarp.org

Center for Retirement Research at Boston College
http://crr.bc.edu/index.php

Certified Financial Planner board of Governors
www.cfp.net

Clifton StrengthsFinder
www.strengthsfinder.com

Congressional Budget Office
http://www.cbo.gov/

Economic Policy Institute
www.epi.org

Employee Benefit Research Institute
http://www.ebri.org/

Families and Work Institute
http://familiesandwork.org

(Board of Governors of the) Federal Reserve System
http://www.federalreserve.gov/

Financial Industry Regulatory Authority (FINRA)
www.finra.org

Financial Planning Association
www.fpaforfinancialplanning.org

Generation Jones:
www.generationjones.com

Myers Briggs
www.myersbriggs.org/.

National Center for Health Statistics
http://www.cdc.gov/nchs/

National Foundation for Credit Counseling
www.nfcc.org

New York Stock Exchange
www.NYSE.com

Occupational Information Network (O*Net)
http://online.onetcenter.org

Retirement 20/20™
www.retirement2020.com

Rutgers University
www.rutgers.edu

Social Security Administration
www.ssa.gov

Standard and Poor's
www.standardandpoors.com/home/en/us

U.S. Census Bureau
http://www.census.gov

US Department of Labor
http://www.dol.gov/

U.S. Department of Labor - Bureau of Labor Statistics
http://www.bls.gov

U.S. Department of the Treasury
http://www.www.ustreas.gov/

U.S. Securities and Exchange Commission
www.sec.gov

University of Michigan
www.umich.edu

Urban Institute
www.urban.org

World Health Organization
http://www.who.int/en/

World Values Survey
http://www.worldvaluessurvey.org/

ORDER FORM
Rethinking Retirement

$19.95 + 2.50 (S&H)

online at:
http://Rethinking-Retirement.com
http://Retirement2020.com
or http://EarlyRetirementHelp.com

by phone:
have your credit card handy and call:
(303) 794-8888

by fax:
(720) 863-2013

by mail:
send check payable to:
Thornton Publishing, Inc.
17011 Lincoln Ave. #408
Parker, Colorado 80134

If it is temporarily sold out at your favorite bookstore,
have them order more of ISBN: 0-9845417-2-1

Name: ____________________
Address: ____________________
____
Phone: ____________________
E-mail: ____________________

Credit Card #: ____________________
Card Type: __________ Expiration Date: ____/ ____
Security Code: ________